GOD'S MOVE – YOUR MOVE

God's Move – Your Move

DECLAN FLANAGAN

KINGSWAY PUBLICATIONS
EASTBOURNE

Copyright © Declan Flanagan 1988

First published 1988

All rights reserved.
No part of this publication may be reproduced or
transmitted in any form or by any means, electronic
or mechanical, including photocopy, recording, or any
information storage or retrieval system, without
permission in writing from the publisher.

Biblical quotations are from the
Holy Bible: New International Version,
copyright © International Bible Society 1973, 1978, 1984.

Front cover photo: Tony Stone Photolibrary—London

British Library Cataloguing in Publication Data
Flanagan, Declan
God's move your move.
1. Witness bearing (Christianity)
I. Title
248'.5   BV4520

ISBN 0–86065–510–5

Printed in Great Britain for
KINGSWAY PUBLICATIONS LTD
Lottbridge Drove, Eastbourne, E. Sussex BN23 6NT by
Cox & Wyman Ltd, Reading.
Typeset by Watermark, Hampermill Cottage, Watford WD14PL

Contents

Preface

The only way that the estimated 2.8 billion people who have not heard the claims of Christ can be reached, is through the whole church being mobilized. Many Christians feel discouraged and defeated in their personal evangelism. They know that Christians are supposed to witness, but how do you go about it? Do you have to be a specialist in evangelism? What do you say? Is evangelism primarily our work or God's work? The Enemy has been busy turning us inwards and having us concentrate on secondary matters. Meanwhile, lost people remain lost.

Reaching out with the gospel is not high on the agenda for many Christians. At a recent major conference, crowds could be seen queueing for seminars dealing with aspects of the supernatural. Seats were easy to find in seminars dealing with mission. Being consistent in our living and witnessing is demanding and there are no simple solutions.

World Christian Magazine (7/85), estimates that most Christians give about 2.4% of their income to Missions. Some denominations donate less than 1% of their income to overseas work. In Britain, 60% of Missionary Societies are in financial difficulty. By 1994, more than 30,000 missionaries worldwide will retire. There are only about 5,000 who are likely to take their places. The present situation is an urgent one.

How does God view our attitudes and actions? His heart pulsates with the desire for lost people. As you discover the Father's heart you cannot fail to notice his commitment to the task of mission. Jesus was a missionary. God has a plan and wants us to co-operate with him. This book seeks to focus on God. We will be looking at what he has done and requires us to do. It is written particularly for those starting out in the Christian life, who want to have a doctrinal and practical understanding of evangelism. We will be observing how God's plan for salvation is developed throughout the Bible. At the end of each chapter are questions and follow up exercises for individual or group use. Select the ones that will be most helpful to you.

Writing this book has been profoundly disturbing. I have been happy to encourage others to consider their involvement in mission. Many sermons and seminars have been given. People have been challenged. Some are now pastors, evangelists and missionaries. I had always thought that those who preach should be prepared to go themselves, but hoped that it would never be me.

While writing the chapter on Jonah, whom I call 'The Reluctant Mover', God started to show me that it was time to leave the affluent, leafy suburbs of south-west London. The last place I ever expected to be sent was Dublin. This was the city where I spent the first seven years of my life. My Nineveh turned out to be Dublin. God's plans cannot be stopped and he made all the arrangements to transfer another reluctant mover.

Thanks are due to those at Cheam Baptist Church and Grosvenor Road Baptist Church, who have 'consumer tested' much of the material in this book. Their patience, along with that of June, Mark and Peter, who wondered what I was doing for so long in the study, has been a source of great encouragement.

If this book helps you to face the challenge of sharing the Father's heart for Mission, I would rejoice with you.

Whether it is where you are now, or somewhere else in the world, is not the crucial question. Evangelism starts where you are now. The Lord who said, 'You will be my witnesses in Jerusalem, and in all Judea and Samaria, and to the ends of the earth' (Acts 1:8) is coming back. His final words stress the importance of the task. When Christ returns, he will want to know if we did what we were told to do.

DECLAN FLANAGAN
Grosvenor Road Baptist Church, Dublin

Part One

God's Move

1

The Rescue Station

The coastline of Britain can be a dangerous place—especially for the summer visitor. While instructing a group of novice canoeists one hot afternoon, I was involved in two unexpected rescue operations. A middle-aged man, totally unaware of the dangers, followed a ball out to sea. Thinking that he was still an athletic twenty years old, he rapidly became exhausted. He had to receive an uncomfortable lift to shore on the back of a canoe.

A few minutes later we were involved again, this time with a five-year-old girl. She had been playing quietly at the water's edge on a rubber lilo. Becoming more adventurous, she waded out into deeper water, totally unaware of the outgoing tide and off-shore winds. Within minutes, she was nearly a mile out to sea and holding on to the lilo with a firm grip. My group of heroic canoeists prepared for another rescue. As we went to help the girl, we were nearly given an early bath from the wash of a high-powered speedboat that had joined in on the action. It was the girl's parents, who had been out to sea enjoying themselves. Without a word of gratitude, they picked up the girl and headed for the crowded beach. 'These things happen,' was their only comment.

Every day similar situations occur. Many people are totally unaware of the physical dangers they face. It is

equally true in the spiritual area of our lives. People set out
to go to work or do the shopping but never return. There
is an inevitability about this happening, but a 'sadly, these
things happen' attitude, is no answer for spiritually lost
and helpless people.

The Christian has been given the responsibility of being
involved in rescue missions. We are not to sit sunning ourselves on the beach when people are drowning in the sea.
My friends and I could have been so concerned about similar people in difficulty at sea, that we set up a permanent
rescue station. We would suddenly become aware that
life-saving is a year-round occupation. Potential drown-
ings and shipwrecks do not occur at specified intervals.
The chronicle of events for our rescue station might have
been as follows:

1. Initial enthusiasm

With only one rescue boat and a few canoes, the team of volunteers make an enthusiastic start. The rescue station building is just an inadequate, cold uncomfortable tin hut. There
is a small group keeping a constant watch out to sea. It is
hard, tiring work looking out for lost people, but zeal and
enthusiasm mean that fatigue is hardly noticed.

At this stage, all the volunteers are working happily
together, and some people are regularly being rescued.
Several of those saved begin to work at the rescue centre.
News of certain dramatic rescues draws the attention of
the local and national media. From within the surrounding
area, people are wanting to identify with something successful. They start giving their time and money to support the
new work. No longer is one boat and a few canoes acceptable—only the best in life-saving equipment will do.
Specialist courses on all aspects of rescue work are initiated.
Within three years, a team of highly-capable leaders
emerges. Some of those initially involved are encouraged to
take up less demanding jobs, like making the tea.

2. The growth phase

The old tin hut does not project the right image of a thriving rescue operation. A more comfortable environment is required for the first refuge of those saved from the cold sea. The old army camp beds are removed, and comfortable facilities are provided in a new, enlarged building. Members like meeting there when not on duty, partly because the club atmosphere is so enjoyable.

3. Growing self-satisfaction

Being a thriving venture, the members become increasingly self-satisfied. There is laughter, fun and plenty of mutual back-slapping. The flags still fly with the rescue station motif proudly displayed. Those who are large financial supporters are given a free tie with motif, for promotional purposes. One of the original members who had maintained his desire to rescue people at sea, notices that the boat is hardly ever launched now. There are rumours that a new firm specializing in rescues will be employed on a part-time basis. This will allow members more opportunity to make money and enjoy themselves.

Around this time, a major accident occurs—a large ship is wrecked off the coast. The hired crews bring in many cold, wet and half-drowned people. Some are sick. Some have different coloured skins. Our happy little club is thrown into chaos. People are taken outside to be cleaned up in case they make a mess everywhere. 'Surely people must be clean before coming inside,' shouts the Chairman, as he sees his life's work turning into a disaster area.

4. Division

A special meeting is hastily called by club members. Everyone expects a full turn out when there is a crisis, and the members willingly oblige. The majority want to cease being a rescue station, as some unpleasant things have happened recently. Some rather undesirable people have been admitted who are hindering the normal social life of the club. Members do not like change, unless it is to make them more comfortable.

Some members insist that the club was designed as a rescue station and that it exists in order to save lives. Following much heated argument, it is decided to terminate all rescue activities until further notice. Those who want to save the lives of all kinds of people, can go and do so elsewhere. They do!

5. Initial enthusiasm followed by endless repeats

The new group has a tremendous start. In their first year, they save over forty lives. After ten years, the number rescued dwindles to just one or two. Those who are saved now have usually made their own way out of the sea, and come to the rescue station because it is warm. One man even comes because there is a poster outside advertising 'Talk on Rescues', followed by coffee. He is cold and thinks that he can put up with the talk if the coffee is good.

As the years go by, the new group sees history repeating itself. The reason for the initial project is soon forgotten. Members are excellent at looking after each other. The door is always open, in case someone cares to come in to be told how to be rescued. Some now think the time has come to start another rescue station, and buy a little tin hut further down the beach.

Should you visit this stretch of coastline today, you will find the tin huts have long gone. In their place are exclusive clubs, catering for like-minded people of the same colour and class. These clubs are almost identical to all the other ones that have taken over the beach. It is even rumoured that a consortium from the Middle East is considering moving in. Shipwrecks are still frequent. Middle-aged men and children on lilos still drown, but the clubs go on for ever.

The church is designed by God to provide a base in the community for rescue activities. We do not exist for our own benefit. Once we become defensive and introspective it is only a short route to closure. Many churches that were prospered by God ten years ago, are now placing FOR SALE notices outside. It was Luis Palau who reminded us that 'the church is only one generation away from extinction'.

When there is the prospect of a terrorist attack, the security services are placed on 'Red Alert'. Dedicated terrorists who are prepared to risk all are capable of creating havoc within minutes. If we are not aware and prepared to resist, the consequences can be devastating. The Enemy of the church has made massive in-roads at key points during this century. Unless we are prepared to resist in the power of the Holy Spirit, he is going to continue his destructive activities. This book is designed to help us recover our confidence in some of the great truths of the Christian gospel. If our gospel is distorted or inadequate at any point, it becomes defensive and lacking in power. Paul was able to say, 'I am not ashamed of the gospel, because it is the power of God for the salvation of everyone who believes' (Romans 1:16).

A fresh examination of the content of our message, with particular emphasis on the character of God, is not merely an academic exercise. It is designed to lead to a deeper appreciation of our Maker, and a response to his claims.

THINK IT THROUGH

Read again the account of the rescue station.
1. At what point do you think the rescue station was most effective?
2. What factors led to its decline?
3. What else, apart from being a rescue station, is the

church designed for?

4. 'What is the church for?' Imagine you have been asked to prepare a two-minute broadcast for local radio, using this heading.

▷ What would you want to say?
▷ How can you ensure that the language and concepts you use are understood by your listeners?

Work on this activity in pairs, and then seek a group consensus. Why not publish your statement in the church magazine and invite others to comment?

5. How can the problems of decline experienced in the rescue station be avoided?

6. What could you do now to help your church develop or maintain an interest in rescue activities?

7. If Satan called a conference of his demons and decided to subvert the truths of Christianity, what would be the particular points of attack? Identify the main aspects and then rank in order of priority.

▷ What success do you think he has been having?
▷ How should we resist? Look at Ephesians 6:10–18.

We must also use our two principal weapons:

▷ Matthew 4:4, 7, 10; Luke 4:4, 8, 12; Ephesians 6:17.
▷ Mark 14:38; Ephesians 6:18.

2

The Outgoing God

Behind the triumphalism evident in some sections of the church today, there is a growing concern that we are seeing little real impact in our evangelism. We delight to hear of:

▷ 1,000 new churches being established each week in Africa.
▷ One quarter of the population of Africa attending church regularly.
▷ One British church in six growing in attendance terms.
▷ Over a quarter of all church-goers in Britain are under fifteen years of age.

While some statistics are very encouraging, when used selectively they can hide the real situation. In Britain and the United States, we as Christians must be concerned about our ineffectiveness in reaching large sectors of society for Christ. We pride ourselves in all the evangelism training programmes, Bible teaching, books, tapes, missions and media ministries. At least fifty Bible publishers in the United States print over 2,670 different Bibles, in thirty-four translations. We are spoilt for choice, while many have none. There has been the tremendous growth of Bible Weeks, conferences and celebrations, yet we should be profoundly disturbed. Valuable

as all these ministries and events are, the tide of godless-
ness is still coming in. Figures available in the *World Christian Encyclopedia* (OUP 1982) and the *UK Christian
Handbook 1985/6* (Marc Europe) reflect the challenge
that faces us in Britain and America:

▷ Between 1970–1980 the United States saw a net
  decline in conversions of 595,000, while in the same
  decade, the Soviet Union recorded a net increase of
  164,000.
▷ In Britain, there has been a decline from 17% of the
  adult population attending church infrequently to
  16%, between 1980 and 1985.
▷ There are 45 million people in the United Kingdom
  who never go to church.
▷ Taking western Europe as a whole, the number of
  practising Christians is projected to fall a further 10%
  before the end of the century.
▷ Child Evangelism report that 90% of the children in
  Britain never attend Sunday School or church.

   Something is wrong. Many answers are suggested and
schemes proposed, but the challenge still faces us. Is it
possible that we think more about our churches and their
activities than we do about God? Many seek to maintain
what they have, and erect 'Do Not Disturb' notices.
Others retreat to a ghetto of their own making and use
their energies on hurling missiles at other Christians, with
whom they disagree on secondary issues. While we are
busily engaged in playing a religious version of *Trivial Pursuits*, the world leaves us to get on with it. Have we done
what has always grieved God—that is, forgotten him?
Does the God revealed in the Bible really have a place in
our thinking and evangelism?
   Several of my family are involved in selling and marketing. They assure me that given the right techniques, you can
sell almost anything. Once the individual is convinced they
need your product, they are likely to purchase. If our think-

ing on evangelism is dominated by the individual's needs and how they can be met, it is relatively easy to convince someone that Christianity will provide all they are looking for. Starting from the basis of need, we may reduce the gospel to a commodity requiring packaging and marketing. It may be presented on a low cost easy plan, which will appeal to those seeking a cosy and comfortable religion. As long as the blessings outweigh the demands, the pill of comfortable Christianity may be easily swallowed.

The first Christians were the radicals of their day. The marketing men would have had difficulty in promoting their cause. Nevertheless, they challenged individuals and society on God's behalf, changing the face of the western world within 300 years. Their own personal requirements had to become secondary in order to serve their Maker. Having yielded their allegiance to Jesus Christ, and taken up their cross, there could be no turning back. These were people who knew their God and were not going to leave him when the going was tough. Today an 'easy come' gospel rapidly becomes an 'easy go' gospel. Eliminating the demands of discipleship does not make Christianity more attractive. People are not so gullible as to believe that following the example of Jesus is easy.

The essence of any relationship is knowledge. Without correct information, it is difficult to establish meaningful contact with anyone. When it comes to knowing and appreciating God, it is vital we know as much as possible about him. As our understanding increases, we find it important to keep in balance God's various attributes. When we fail to do this, our concept of God becomes lopsided. Some Christians who delight in the holiness of God to the exclusion of his intimate love, may end up with a God who is remote and takes little interest in the affairs of his creation. The current tendency to have a God there to meet our every need, reduces our Maker to existing for our sole benefit. Balance is important.

Moving house can be an expensive business. To reduce

the cost and do it yourself can be an attractive proposition, especially if you have some gullible friends! My first attempt at moving nearly ended up as an expensive disaster. In wanting to complete this exercise in hard labour as quickly as possible, I paid no attention to equally distributing the weight in the removal van. All the heavy items ended up on the same side. Being overloaded on one side meant that driving the van was extremely difficult. The creaking sound from the back axle indicated that it was not enjoying the experience either.

Today we must beware of the danger of being out of balance. We tend to speak of all the benefits of being a Christian, without stressing God's requirements for holy living. In our zeal to meet the pressing needs of so many people, we can underestimate the character of God and the demands of the gospel. This misleads people into thinking they know the God of the Bible, when all they have discovered is a God of their own making.

The poet Gordon Bailey illustrates the tendency to find a Jesus who will be acceptable to all:

Will the real Jesus please get lost

I like to think of Jesus as a decent sort of chap,
you know the sort of character I mean:
he's neither God in human form, nor is he just a myth,
but someone sort of somewhere in between.
He's meek and mild, a good example, talks a lot of sense,
a help when other help cannot be found;
a universal balsam who can soothe a troubled soul;
a handy sort of bloke to have around.[1]

A failure to appreciate God as he truly is, leads to little faith, weak worship and no real power for living.

If you were to ask the friend who helped me to unpack the furniture van, 'What was inside?' he could tell you every item, because he carried most of them! It would take him a long time to name each one, so to make things easier he would use the collective word 'furniture'. The word 'God' is a composite word, and we need to start unpacking it. As we do so, we need to bear in mind the words of John Calvin: 'God, to keep us sober, speaks sparingly of his essence.' We are never going to understand fully the character of God. There is always going to be more to discover. In making our observations, we may become acquainted with his activities, and want to share in them.

The Bible does not start with establishing the existence of God. It simply announces: 'In the beginning God ...' (Genesis 1:1). We are not told the intellectual route to take in order to be certain God exists. Bonhoeffer rightly said: 'A God who let us prove his existence would be an idol.' God's existence is assumed as the Bible's first certainty. From there, it helps us to discover all we can about him. Cicero, writing in 45 BC said, 'You do not see God, nevertheless, you recognize him from his works.' Our observations of God may lead us towards faith. Proof comes at the end, as a result of examination and action. It bears the nature of confirmation, not of discovery.

The initiator of contact between God and man, is God himself. We can know him because he is self-revealing. There is a sense in which God cannot keep quiet about himself. He desires contact with the objects of his special act of creation: men and women. We should not think so much of people discovering God, but God making himself known to men. Without God taking the initiative, it would be impossible for us to acquire any knowledge of him. He is not passive, waiting for us to have some 'spiritual brainwave' on a good day, that will convince us of his existence and love. All our knowledge of God is derived from his self-revelation. Without it, we are lost.

The nature of God

At this stage we must ask, 'What is God like? Is he an impersonal force, an influence, a philosophy to be thought out or a person to be known?' We can, through revelation, discover:

God is personal

He is not like the giant robots employed in car factories, totally programmed and devoid of the ability to think for themselves. He is capable of independent thinking, strong emotions and determined actions: 'I am the Lord, who exercises kindness, justice and righteousness on earth, for in these I delight' (Jeremiah 9:24).

God is tri-personal

There is only one personal God, but he has revealed himself in three distinct persons: the Father, the Son and the Holy Spirit. We find this difficult to understand and human explanations are inadequate. There are not three separate individuals (as if there were three gods), but three divine persons within the one deity. The unity of God is vital. God has no parts occupied by different persons. Wherever God is, all three persons are present. In 2 Corinthians 13:14, Father, Son and Spirit are brought together in one verse: 'May the grace of the Lord Jesus Christ, and the love of God, and the fellowship of the Holy Spirit be with you all.'

When someone becomes a Christian, each divine person of the Godhead is involved:

The Father is the author of salvation (John 6:37, 44; Ephesians 1:4–5, 11–12) and sends the Son to be our Saviour (John 1:16–17).

The Son is God with us and for us

▷ He has authority to forgive sins (Mark 2:5).
▷ He possessed exhaustive and definitive knowledge of God (Matthew 11:27).
▷ He asserted an eternal existence (John 1:1; 8:23).
▷ He is confessed as eternally divine (John 1:1–4; Philippians 2:6; Colossians 1:15–17).

The Spirit brings to us our salvation. He is a person. Not a force or an 'it'.

▷ He can be grieved (Ephesians 4:30), lied to (Acts 5:3–4) and provoked (Acts 5:9).

▷ He is sent by the Son, from the Father, to testify about Christ (John 15:26). When the main character of a play appears in the centre of the stage, the spotlight is firmly placed on him. The Holy Spirit highlights the person and work of Christ. He is also acting as 'matchmaker' to bring together the faithful Father and the estranged son.

▷ The Holy Spirit can help us come to our senses, like the lost son in the parable told by Jesus.

▷ He is convicting the world of guilt in regard to sin and righteousness and judgement (John 16:8).

▷ He performs personal acts and functions. He is called the 'Paraclete' in John 14 and 16. This title was used of the advocate in the law courts and includes ministries of being Counsellor, Comforter, Friend, Witness and Remembrancer.

▷ He dwells in the Christian, and brings us to the full personality and love of God (Romans 5:5).

God is eternal

He has always existed. If he had been created, he would owe his existence to another who would be greater. He was neither the product of an evolving consciousness or dependent on any other (Acts 17:25; Psalm 90:2). He is independent. His wisdom was not discovered in text books. His power was not developed or acquired. It has always been there, and always will be.

God is infinite

Infinity for humans, locked in time and space, is difficult to contemplate. We are like a single cell attempting to understand the complexities of how the brain works, and the way it came into existence. Infinity is strange.

▷ An infinite being is God.
▷ Infinite time is eternity—God is eternal (Psalm 90:2).
▷ Infinite knowledge is omniscience—God knows all things (Psalm 139:1–12).
▷ Infinite power is omnipotence—God has all power (Genesis 17:1).
▷ Infinite existence is omnipresence—God is everywhere (Psalm 139:7–12).
▷ Infinite love is agape—God is love (1 John 4:8).

God is holy

God's holiness is central to his being. He is completely without fault. There is no inherent defect that could make him fail. His holiness means he is distinct from all he has created. He alone is God. As he is utterly pure and perfect, truthful and just, good and righteous, he must resist and oppose that which is not. He requires his people to share the quality of holiness: 'Be holy, because I am holy' (Leviticus 11:44).

God rules

God's authority is exercised over all the universe. He controls all the elements within it. Fully aware of all that happens he can never be taken by surprise. There is never a day when he is unavailable because of holiday, or tiredness. God is in control of all the events of life, even when evil confronts us. 'Our God is in heaven; he does whatever pleases him' (Psalm 115:3).

The Bible has much more to tell us about the nature of God. Within him is the perfect blending of holiness and love, wrath and mercy, justice and grace, meekness and majesty. He does not merely possess love, he *is* love. His love is shown in all his attitudes and actions. God desires that these qualities be part of his people. As we appreciate the nature of God, it helps us deal with real situations. George Matheson, who wrote many hymns in the latter part of the nineteenth century, was faced with the prospect of going blind. At the time he was engaged to be married and he told his fiancée of the imminent blindness. Her response almost crushed him as she returned the engagement ring to him, and the marriage was called off. Turning to the God he knew, from the despair of that situation, he was able to write:

> O love that wilt not let me go,
> I rest my weary soul in thee,
> I give thee back the life I owe,
> That in thine ocean depths its flow
> May richer, fuller be.

For George Matheson, the knowledge of God was not dry and academic. We may not know the meaning of omnipotence and omnipresence, but we can know the truth of Romans 8:31, 'If God is for us, who can be against us?' and, 'Our God stands in our defence.'

In our evangelism, we want people to encounter the true God, not some cheap imitation. If we know him well, we will have greater confidence in him.

Tracking down God

Should you have ever sought to follow the tracks of a wild animal, you will know that close observation is vital. At times, progress is easy because the tracks are clearly defined. You may, of course, totally lose them. Evidence that God is making himself known can be found as we observe the tracks he has placed for us. They can be found in:

Creation

Paul, in Romans 1:20, is convinced that 'since the creation of the world God's invisible qualities ... have been clearly seen, being understood from what has been made, so that men are without any excuse'. It is taught in John 1:18 and

Hebrews 11:27, that God is invisible, but Paul is saying his
qualities have been clearly seen. What can he mean? How
is it possible to see the unseen? Our physical eyes are
unable to see all God's invisible qualities, but are quite
capable of observing the beauty and order within creation.
While our eyes are observing the glory of the created universe, the soul, with its capacity for deeper contact with
God can be impressed. It may clearly see that God's power
is displayed 'from what has been made'.

Nature is no longer perfect because of the fall. It has its
cruel and ruthless aspects as well as its beautiful ones. The
perfect creation has been flawed, and waits with mankind
to be redeemed (Romans 8: 20, 21). The observation of
nature itself will never lead us all the way to God, but like
a good signpost, it may point us in the right direction.

Conscience

Many modern motor cars are fitted with hazard warning
lights. They do not come on automatically, but a button
has to be pressed in order for the lights to flash. Once acti-
vated, the lights start flashing to warn of danger. God has
placed an early-warning system in people, which he acti-
vates. We may not want to respond to the warning being
given, but unless we deliberately intend to ignore it, he has
a way of alerting us. Obviously our background and
environmental factors are going to influence our decisions, but we still find a basic awareness of matters being
either right or wrong. We can imagine that we have no
conscience, but find it still plays an important part in determining attitudes and actions.

Our consciences are not only early warning devices.
Within the next few years there will be a new breed of
computer-controlled cars. If you want to go to a certain
destination, you will feed into the computer the correct
information and it will select the best route for you. The
conscience can act as an inner guide, to keep us on the
right route. It can help us to avoid potential hazards on the

way, and enable us to arrive at our ultimate destination.

Paul, in his consideration of law and judgement in Romans 2, declares that God has shown his requirements in the giving of the law. Although people may not acknowledge the God who gave the law, they 'do by nature things required by the law' (verse 14). The communication of the requirements of God are there 'since they show that the requirements of the law are written on their hearts, their consciences also bearing witness' (verse 15).

Sin has caused our consciences to be distorted. For example, we do not always recognize the warning signals, rather like the man driving his car on the motorway at an excessive speed. He fails to observe the flashing warning lights ahead of him and only slows down when it is too late. The resulting mess for himself and others, is testimony to his stupidity. In Acts 14:17, Paul informs the unbelievers at Lystra, that '[God] has not left himself without testimony'. God communicates an awareness that we have a responsibility to do good and keep away from evil. If we fail to act on what God is saying, there are consequences here and now. Ultimately we will meet our Maker, to whom we are finally responsible.

History

The relation of God to the everyday life of men is not always plain or easy to understand. The Old Testament records the inevitable effects of what happens when good and evil co-exist together: people suffer. It is sometimes difficult to understand how some of the terrible events recorded there, and some still happening today, correspond to the love and grace of God. Frequently the prophets and poets appear puzzled by events. God's activity may be discerned, but not always understood by our finite minds. The prophet Jeremiah brings his concern to God as he seeks to make sense of events around him: 'You are always righteous, O Lord, when I bring a case before you. Yet I would speak with you about your justice: Why does the way of the wicked prosper?' (Jeremiah 12:1). He opens his heart to God and receives some partial answers. God himself shares the prophet's sorrow. He is concerned that his ways are opposed and that the people have roared against him like a lion would (verse 8). Any opposition to God has consequences. Jeremiah, following his enquiry, comes to the conviction that God has a gracious purpose in the troubles that have been so disturbing.

Alongside those with little regard for God, we find throughout history God's supporters standing for a better way, often at great personal cost. People such as Martin Luther, John Wesley, William Wilberforce, Martin Luther King and Alexander Solzhenitsyn have made their mark in the events of history, for God.

Marxist historians tell us that events in history result from the struggles of nations and classes. There is an inevitable, predictable pattern which continues to repeat itself. God does not exist, so everything has a natural explanation. Such confidence in detecting an orderly pattern in history takes a great deal of faith. There are many unknown factors that could have changed the course of world events. Would the western world be different if the assassination attempt on Ronald Reagan had succeeded? What if the small minority opposed to Hitler had been able to stop him? History does not reflect regular patterns, but a series of events involving real people, with their own particular characteristics. Looking back, we can see the results of greed, exploitation and sin which affected people.

In the Old Testament, God is seen as active. He is there leading his people out of Egypt, strengthening them in their battles, influencing their decisions, while demanding high standards of allegiance and behaviour. Should people fail to remember their Creator, the consequences could be disastrous. God does not stand idly by in the face of exploitation, injustice and greed. Biblical history allows us to observe God's activity in dealing severely with situations, in order that they might improve.

Through the events of our day, God is seeking to communicate. Observing specifically his activity may at times be difficult, but an understanding of God's nature and his activities in the past, will help us to detect his involvement today. He does not stand idly by when people forsake him and fail to live by his standards. God controls the sequence of events, and fulfils his purposes at all times. He can use men and nations who are not even conscious that they are carrying out part of a divine plan.

An understanding of God may be developed through creation, conscience and his activity in history, but if this were all the information we had available, our conception of God would be severely limited. It would be like trying to find a man dressed in grey clothes on a foggy night. The fog begins to clear and the knowledge of God increases as we note his communication in:

The Bible

Standing on top of a snow-capped mountain in the Swiss Alps, is a breathtaking experience. Should you try to write, describing those moments, to someone who has seen only the pinnacles of the city sky-scraper, you soon realize how difficult it is. If that person also speaks a foreign language, the task is even more demanding. Communicating a mountain-top experience is almost impossible, but we can attempt this by using language. God allows us to know something of what he is like, because he has spoken to us. 'All Scripture is God-breathed' (2 Timothy 3:16).

The idea of inspiration is basic to our whole understanding of the Bible. Within the Bible we have a permanent and reliable record of all God wanted to reveal. God's primary authorship of the Bible makes it a unique book. We are to approach it with a willingness to recognize that God speaks through it and calls us to submit to its teaching. The Holy Spirit, who inspired the writers, enables us to understand them today. It is vital that we carefully examine the original setting and intended meaning of a particular section of the Bible, before applying it to today. This will involve us in study and use of the tools of biblical interpretation. Such applications will be richly rewarded as we discover that the Bible speaks today.

The Bible is God's way of communicating with us. In it, he shares his thoughts and purposes with us. The words in the Bible were originally spoken and written to particular people at a given time. God sought to express himself in ways that people could understand. He spoke powerfully and unmistakably through the prophets in specific situations. The record contained in the Bible, traces the whole of God's dealings from creation to the cross and beyond. It takes us to the cross and concludes with the prospect of new heavens and earth. Without the Bible, we would know nothing of God's master plans for redemption and renewal.

Today God's words, given through the Bible authors, can speak powerfully to people. The problems of receiving and doing what God requires are not fundamentally associated with communication, as many would suggest. It was Mark Twain who said, 'There are many things in the Bible that I do not understand. It's the ones that I do understand that bother me.' At the very heart of the Bible is Jesus Christ, the One who met all the demands of his Father. The Bible is a history of God's rescue operations in the past.

The word of God, taken by the Spirit of God, continues to have a dynamic quality. It changes people's lives. Terrorists, thieves, intellectuals, strong, weak, black or white, on reading the Bible with an open mind, find God is still speaking.

A barrow-boy, at Billingsgate fish market in London, decided to become a follower of Jesus Christ. Within a few weeks, he was asked to read the Bible at the morning service in the local Anglican Church which he had started attending. He introduced the reading with: 'Here you lot, button your ears back and listen. This is really good stuff!' The vicar was a little surprised, but relieved that the introduction did not contain a few of the choice words frequently heard at Billingsgate but rarely in church. As with all disciples of Christ, this young man had areas of his life that needed to change, but his conviction that the Bible is 'good stuff' was very refreshing.

The Bible does not treat its heroes like the glossy good guys and girls in the TV soap operas. Their questions, problems, doubts and failures are all open to inspection. Nothing is hidden. People with similar difficulties to ourselves are there to observe. Their deepest needs are uncovered as they seek love, life and forgiveness.

God has spoken and is still speaking through the Bible, the most remarkable of books. In it we can learn about God, about ourselves and the way in which we can enter a relationship together. God has taken the initiative. He has spoken. The Bible itself is not to be worshipped— neither creation nor the Bible can save us. This can only come about through:

Jesus Christ

Jesus appeared quietly among the Jewish people. This was the fullest revelation of all. Following the initial disturbances caused by Herod at his birth, events go quiet for thirty years. Jesus eventually burst onto the scene, speaking about God and man. He did not come proposing a new doctrine of God or suggesting that people's previous knowledge needed a total revolution. Like any good teacher, he started where people were in their conception of God and freed it from the excessive religious shackles that well-meaning people had placed on it. He gave a richer understanding of God. He was able to take the best Jewish teaching available and further enrich people's understanding.

No longer was God to be a matter of speculation. He had arrived on earth personally. 'The Word became flesh and lived for a while among us' (John 1:14). His teaching is not a matter of speculation, but of life. The knowledge of God is totally different from the knowledge frequently required to pass an examination: once learned, soon forgotten! With Jesus, truth understood and received is to lead to eternal life. He is seeking not just information about, but acquaintance with, his Father. God is to be known by living in right relationship with him. A person is to know God as a child knows his parents: through birth. Birth leads to a family relationship which is to be experienced and enjoyed.

W.N. Clarke wrote:

> According to Jesus, God is to be known not by theory, but by practice, not through mental investigation, but through spiritual trust and fellowship. Only a son can know the Father. The consequence of this is that the knowledge of God is available to children and to all whom God chooses to reveal Himself.[2]

It was Christ's mission to bring men into the experience of God which he richly enjoyed. Jesus did not regard a relationship with his Father so unusual that nobody else could share it. Christ is still the living Word, and as such he can be known and enjoyed in a personal way.

God has spoken in a general sense through creation, conscience and history. Specifically, God has made himself known with even greater clarity in Jesus, the eternal Word of God and through the Bible. The Bible declares the Christ we know in our personal experience. There can be no other Christ, unless he is a product of our imagination. If we want to properly interpret the Bible, we need to do so from the perspective of the living Christ. He is the central theme of the Bible from beginning to end. God's purposes are declared in Christ and are discovered by us through repentance and faith in him.

God is still seeking to make himself known to his creation. At times, he may communicate dramatically and through supernatural means. Missionaries have for many years been letting us know of miraculous happenings as the gospel has penetrated new areas. Accompanying the message have frequently been events that could only be described as supernatural. Are we beginning to see a movement into areas of Britain that are under the domination of Satan? If we are, some unusual things may happen, which will indicate that God is active and still speaking. We should not discount the possibility of supernatural events confirming the message already given in the Bible.

THINK IT THROUGH

1. What do you find most convincing evidence for the existence of the outgoing God?

2. In your communication with unbelievers, what would you particularly emphasize, to establish the existence of God?

3. Study carefully Paul's defence of the faith in Acts 17. What arguments does he use?

4. What do you find encouraging and discouraging as you consider the statistics included in this chapter?

5. In what ways do you observe the church playing *Trivial Pursuits*?

6. Suppose a friend wrote to you asking what God was like. In a few paragraphs seek to prepare a reply that explains something of the God you know.

3

The Evangelizing God

'Come, Gentlemen, we sit too long on trifles' (Shakespeare, Pericles, II, iii).

In the moment taken to read this sentence, someone will have gone to face their Maker. Meanwhile, the church maintains an outstanding ability to sit on trifles. The new religious craze of trifle sitting is enjoyable, but a little uncomfortable when faced with really important issues. The months can go by, but little seems to happen. We may succeed in altering the colour, or administering the change of location, between the jelly and the fruit, but essentially the trifle remains the same. The majority of the population are content to leave us to get on with it. Any enthusiasm is not welcomed as it has the tendency of disturbing the status quo. Thankfully, God is not inactive and is concerned for the spiritual state of those whom he has created. He is constantly calling people to himself and desires that his followers cease their trifle sitting activities. The disciples of Christ are to be active participants in sharing the good news with people.

Our God is a missionary God. Christian mission did not begin with the incarnation or Pentecost, but has its origins in the character of God. If God's heart did not burn for lost people, there would have been no incarnation or Pentecost.

In the Old Testament we can observe God's willingness to be involved in the lives of individuals.

Adam and Eve

The depth of relationship that existed between God, Adam and Eve, is beyond our understanding. Walking together in the garden must have been a delight. Apart from the beautiful surroundings, being able to speak without fear of contradiction and misunderstanding, would have brought deep contentment. God, who had been the initiator of the relationship, found joy in personal communication.

Having created the earth and heavens, God was at that stage not satisfied. The task was incomplete. What God made was good, but he wanted it to be very good. Nothing had been spoiled. No cross word was uttered and no tear had been shed. Yet, there was still something lacking. There was nobody to enjoy what God had made. At that point, God stooped and made man. Now all was very good. God could rest from his creative work.

God had created man in his own image, capable of feeling the intimacy and love of his Maker. Man is the last link between creation and Creator and is capable of deep communion with God. The relationship depends on trust and obedience. Adam, having been made in the image of God, was capable of making independent decisions. He was given freedom to eat the fruit of any tree except the tree 'of the knowledge of good and evil, for when you eat of it you will surely die' (Genesis 2:17). This minor prohibition indicated that we are not free to do exactly as we want in this world. Certain moral restrictions are there for our benefit.

Further provision was made by God in the form of Eve. Together they could share intimacy, thought and conversation with one another and with God. Adam and Eve must have been full of devotion and praise. They had been created by God. They were the sole occupants of Paradise. However, although filled with joy, they gave in to temptation, and ate from the forbidden tree. Having eaten from the tree, they knew the relationship of trust and obedience had been broken. Now there was the dread of meeting with God. They experienced a deep sense of loss and attempted to conceal themselves from God. Having been made for close communion with God, seeking to withdraw must have been a totally unnatural experience. It was also totally irrational. Their knowledge of God must have told them that it was impossible to hide from the all-seeing God. Furthermore, there was the shame of their nakedness and their inability to do anything to help themselves.

In Genesis 3:9, we see the first example of God's great heart of love reaching out to lost people. 'The Lord God called to the man, "Where are you?"' The first question of the Bible cannot merely be a desire for information. God knew where the couple were hiding.

God's heart is saddened as he realizes that perfection has been marred by disobedience. All God's plans for earth were to be established through Adam and Eve, but they had spoilt it. They were to take their orders only from God, but now they had let him down. Adam and Eve were not only created by God, but *for* God. Their Maker was to enjoy their company. The question provided the opportunity for the restoration of the relationship. It was an intelligible question that could be understood and answered correctly with a confession of guilt. Instead, excuses were made. For God to come and look for the two hiding in the garden is a mark of his grace. He could have disowned them, and left them to follow their own sinful path.

God's act in creation could have told us only a little about him. There is infinitely more to God than wisdom and the power to create. In God himself coming to look for Adam and Eve, we see his holiness, his mercy, his love, his tenderness, his patience and his goodness. These could only really be noted following a breaking of trust and obedience. God acted initially to create, now he had to set in motion a process to save. God's coming to Adam clearly demonstrated that man was helpless and totally lost. Why should God come to seek? Why should he even consider restoring what was lost? Why should he be willing to meet with those who disobeyed? Surely, only because he is love.

From Genesis 3, we observe two tracks developing in the Bible. One illustrates the consequences of the fall; the other leads to Christ.

The consequences of the fall

For Satan

Satan had made himself out to be man's friend and God as man's enemy, so he was cursed and made an object of contempt. No questions were asked of Satan because it was not possible for him to repent. His misery was irreversible. He could no longer even be the apparent friend of mankind, but his open enemy. Satan seeks to destroy all that is good and all that is possible through God. One day, he will be finally defeated. The fall of Adam and Eve exposed all people subsequently to the fierce antagonism of Satan. It means that Christians must be prepared to be soldiers involved in a battle, using spiritual weapons. Having a pleasant time, sitting on trifles in the face of such an enemy, will not do.

For woman

The command had already been given, 'Be fruitful and increase in number' (Genesis 1:28). Now this was going to involve pain in childbirth. Sin is the cause of physical suffering in the world. Part of Eve's punishment for listening to Satan and accepting his authority rather than God's, was that she became subject to her husband's rule (3:16).

It has been man's tendency to dominate and abuse women. The willingness in many different cultures to treat

women as slaves is a consequence of the fall. The headship
of man within Christian marriage, is to be based on love
(Ephesians 5:25), not on the domination which originates
from the fall. Today, when there is much debate about
women's role in society and the church, we must
remember the origin of the situation. It will help us to
remember that the purpose of redemption is to restore the
situation between God and men, and between men and
women, as it existed before the fall. 'There is neither ...
male nor female, for you are all one in Christ Jesus' (Galatians 3:28). Men and women are equal in status, but different in role.

For man

Some people imagine that work is a consequence of the
fall, and that Adam and Eve lived a life of luxury and ease
until then. They consider that if man had not fallen, we
would all be able to live a life without work. This is a mis-
take and a pleasant dream for those who do not like work.
Jerome said, 'I like work: it fascinates me. I can sit and
look at it for hours. I love to keep it by me: The idea of getting rid of it nearly breaks my heart.'

Adam was busy making a start on the command given:
'Fill the earth and subdue it' (1:28). He had been placed in
the garden to work and take care of it (2:15). He had also
been busy gathering food and naming the animals. There
was certainly work to do in Paradise, but it was different
from work today. He would have experienced total job
satisfaction. There would have been no executive stress
and strain, and no headaches at the end of the day.

Following the fall, the ground was cursed and was to
resist man's authority over it. In taking the fruit, he gave
up his rulership over creation. Now hard work and effort
are required to produce anything. The earth was changed
in its relationship to man. There were to be thorns and
thistles (3:18) to frustrate his purposes. Sweat would be
required to produce anything worth while.

The final punishment was for him to return to the ground from which he had been made. God had said, 'You must not touch it, or you will die.' That happened spiritually. As soon as he sinned, Adam lost the intimate contact with God, although he continued to live on physically. God was still capable of working out his purposes through him.

Sin is serious. We must not trifle with it. The effects are seen throughout the world today. It was Karl Marx who said, 'Original sin is everywhere at work.' Man is lost and totally unable to help himself. He is excluded from Paradise. Something had to be done to restore what had been broken. *God moved*.

Alongside the disastrous events of Genesis 3, the other track may be observed:

The line that leads to Christ

God was fully aware of the helplessness of man. To rectify the situation, he set in action a great rescue plan. Sin and death had to be dealt with. God alone could deal with the situation by coming himself as the Deliverer. The innocent party was the only one capable of offering forgiveness, but it would cost the life of his Son, Jesus. A terrible predicament required a drastic solution. From Genesis 3, we observe the line of descent that would lead to Bethlehem and on to the hill outside Jerusalem. Maybe Eve had hoped that the Deliverer would come immediately and that her first son, Cain, would put right the problem of sin. But she 'brought forth a man' (Genesis 4:1) with the same sinful tendencies of all who would follow. God knew what Cain was really like and confronted him by saying, 'Sin is crouching at your door; it desires to have you, but you must master it' (Genesis 4:7). The problem of sin remained and grew quickly. On his own, he was unable to conquer sin, and he killed his brother, Abel, as a result of anger and jealousy.

Recently, I deposited a pen in the inside pocket of a new jacket. It was a hot day and as the temperature rose the red ink decided it no longer wanted to be constricted within the confines of the pen top. It rapidly soaked the lining of the pocket and soon afterwards, the fabric of the jacket. When I put the jacket on, the ink decided to spread a little further to my new shirt. At this point, my young son, thinking that possibly I had been shot, decided to get in on the act and stick his fingers on the red ink. Within a few minutes, his fingerprints were clearly observable around the house.

Noah

It does not take long for sin to spread. Within a few generations its effects were dominating thousands. The world in which Noah lived bore many similarities to our own:

It was a world in which marriage was abused (Genesis 6:2)

People were living much longer than they do today. Their additional years gave them greater opportunity to sin. The constraints of ageing and the fear of death were not so great. The men observed the beautiful women and chose any they desired. The satisfaction of physical desire was the motivating force. The violation of God's standards in marriage had its consequences then as it does today. Society is weakened.

It was a world dominated by violence (Genesis 6:4)

There were men around at that time of great physical strength and power. Sheer brute force, coupled with great physical energy, made these men the dominant force. The adulation given to 'Rambo' and 'Rocky' today, might compare with the fame of 'The Giants' of Noah's time. These were the popular heroes. They had no concern for the weak or poor. Those who sought good were despised and persecuted. Such men had little regard for the law, because they could rule through force. To seek to rule by physical force is a mark of sin. Any who seek to rule by force will see an increase in violence.

It was a world which God was fully aware of (Genesis 6:5)

'The Lord saw how great man's wickedness on the earth had become, and that every inclination of the thoughts of his heart was only evil all the time.' Today, we can watch any amount of news programmes illustrating graphically the activities of man. But whereas we can only observe from the outside, God's gaze is deeper and he sees the heart.

God saw the actions of man and knew that the source of the problem was deep within. His heart was grieved that he had ever made man in the first place. For God to observe the source and consequences of sin caused him pain. Some action was required.

It was a world threatened by destruction (Genesis 6:6-7)

God had previously shortened man's life span to 120 years (6:3). Now he intended to eradicate sin from the earth. The situation had become so bad that drastic action had to be taken. God continued to be grieved by his creation, but while absolute destruction was contemplated, there was the potential for mercy because of the life of one man, Noah, who was blameless and walked with God.

God's judgement swept through the earth in the form of the flood. He waited until the right time before the flood came. Instructions for the building of the ark were given. This provided a way out for Noah and his family. God noticed Noah and acted to rescue him. Sin had reached a climax and God acted to bring judgement and to save.

God must have soon been saddened again when Noah and his family came out of the ark. The influence of sin remained. A vineyard was planted. Too much wine was consumed and Noah became drunk. His sons shared a joke at his expense and the end result was the cursing of

Shem. In this case, the son was worse off than the guilty father. Sin is infectious and it continues to influence our family and our friends.

The situation remains the same as we move throughout the Old Testament. We continue to find examples of man's sin meeting God's judgement and grace. The Hebrew writers were not men of speculation, but of observation. They observed the effects of sin in the individual and upon society. God's hatred for sin, and his desire to overcome it, are the great themes of the Old Testament.

Babel

In Genesis 11, man's pride caused him to think he could erect a tower at Babel, to reach God. The people were judged, by being scattered throughout the earth, and the problems were compounded as they all spoke different languages.

Grace is observed in God deciding to deal particularly with one race. His selection of Israel was not upon merit, but because he decided to act through them, in order that it would be possible for salvation to be available again for all peoples. God acted through a specially called minority, initiating the relationship and directing affairs.

Abraham

Throughout the Old Testament, God is presented as the Rescuer and his plans are progressively revealed. God promises himself—not to individuals, but to a nation, Israel. The people of Israel have always regarded themselves as a 'special case' because they were selected by God and had a particular relationship with him through the covenant he had made. The making of covenants, or mutually binding contracts, was a common event. It involved two people making binding promises, but in the case of God's covenant with Israel, we see him taking the initiative again. God's character is expressed in his willingness to enter into a covenant based on love. He is moved by the helplessness of the people and reaches out to them, knowing that there was a purpose for Israel which he wished them to carry out. God was not content to live in isolation, but brought about a people for whom he may care and relate to.

The situation had become so bad that any knowledge of God had almost disappeared. The call to Abraham was the first great act of God towards the formation of his church.

The initiative was taken by God (Genesis 12:1)

'The Lord had said....' The call of God is unmistakable. Abraham was pursuing his business interests and looking after his flocks and herds. He had not made a careful study to discover God's plans for him, which he would later obey. The idea of a change of location did not occur to him at a moment of great inspiration. The martyr Stephen, in Acts 7:2, tells that, 'The God of Glory appeared to our father Abraham.' God, with great power, moved into Abraham's life, in order to continue his plans to save lost people. The call came to Abraham without him moving one fraction in the direction of God. God decided to act. In a similar way today, God moves into people's lives. Unless he takes action, there is no possibility in us coming to him.

The requirements were clear (Genesis 12:1)

Abraham was required to leave:

(a) *His security*. This is demanding, as there is no obvious guarantee for the future. Anyone who will follow God's way must first be prepared to leave their present way of life. 'God at first showed his concern by taking from the Gentiles a people for himself' (Acts 15:14). The call of God always involves leaving the past securities behind. Abraham was about to set off into the unknown.

(b) *His country*. For Abraham, this meant literally leaving, severing the geographical and emotional ties with his country. Abraham was clearly an early missionary. He was not a young man wanting the adventures of travel, but a settled, mature seventy-five year old, who quite liked being where he was. The call of God for him meant packing up and moving out, just as it does for those called to missionary work today. There has to be a willingness to leave the comforts of home, along with all the old ambitions and cherished habits.

(c) His home. At home you can be yourself. You can take off your shoes if you want to! Abraham faced a real challenge here and did not move into a position of blessing until his father died. The narrow circle of a happy family is the hardest to leave, because of the close associations that exist. To be prepared to leave loved ones is one of the greatest demands on any missionary, yet Jesus says, 'Anyone who loves his father or mother more than me is not worthy of me' (Matthew 10:37).

The call to leave security, country and home, was a call to leave legitimate and worth-while things. When God calls us to leave legitimate things of this world, he allows us to share something of the experience of his Son, Jesus, who left the security and intimacy of heaven. Being prepared to leave what was good and legitimate in order to accomplish something of lasting value, was God's desire for Abraham, for Christ and for us as his disciples. God calling Abraham out of his present position was not because he was mean and wanted to separate him from all that is enjoyable in life. God had a clear purpose in mind. If Abraham had been unwilling to leave the calm and security of Ur, he would never have received the great blessing that God had for him and his descendants.

The demands required faith
Today we are able to observe many in the past and the pres-

ent who have responded to God's initiative and have been blessed. The example they have set gives us greater confidence than if we were to be the first. What is remarkable about Abraham, is that he had no precedent to follow. He was the 'trail blazer' for others to model themselves on. All Abraham had to go on was the clear sense that God had spoken to him and that there were things to be done. In spite of the cost and personal hazards, '[Abraham] left, as the Lord had told him' (Genesis 12:4).

Abraham had to experience a journey without any clear idea of what might happen to him. Facing unknown circumstances is demanding and we naturally want to retreat from them. We can always find more good reasons for remaining where we are and doing nothing. Faith is the divine energy that can shatter complacency and move us into the unknown. Abraham knew his God and had some awareness of his power. Our faith is not some attachment to a set of theological statements about God, but a confidence in his ability to do what he says he will do. God did not give Abraham a detailed explanation of his reasons, along with the ancient equivalent of an AA route map. Without all the knowledge he would have surely desired, Abraham was prepared to trust God and leave him to work out the details. Faith is dependent on some knowledge and is not an existential leap in the dark. Abraham had a real conviction that it was God who was speaking to him, and was confident that the most reasonable thing to do was to obey.

I am often concerned when it appears that following Christ is a dull, lifeless encounter with a series of regulations designed to make us miserable. When God is leading the way and our confidence is in him, this must be a false representation of what Christianity is all about. Abraham, seventy-five not out, was about to commence the greatest adventure of his life.

The Old Testament is full of examples of God's concern for the safety, survival and welfare of the human race. God is involved. Other biblical events that show us the evangelizing nature of God include:

▷ Abraham's intercession for Sodom and Gomorrah (Genesis 18).
▷ Joseph's influence in Egypt (Genesis 42–47).
▷ Moses and the Exodus (Exodus 1–12).
▷ Mordacai's intervention on behalf of the Jews who appear doomed (Esther 1–10).
▷ Daniel's position of authority enabling him to express God's concern (Daniel 1–6).
▷ Nehemiah's concern for the return of the captives (Nehemiah 1–6).
▷ Naomi's concern for Ruth (Ruth 1–4).

God has always loved the sinner and sought to save him wherever he is. God is an evangelizing God. He has sustained the world for many years, and he desires to save lost people. Those he calls to be his representatives commence the greatest adventure that life can offer.

THINK IT THROUGH

1. Read Genesis 3 tracing the steps that led to the fall. What were the repercussions for

▷ Nature?
▷ The relationship between men and women?
▷. Man's relationship with God?
▷ Man's relationship with nature and the necessity for work?

2. How do you think God felt as he observed the events in Genesis 3?
3. The consequences of one man's sin were enormous. How did God plan to save the situation, and reverse the effects of the fall? (See Romans 5:12–19.)

4. How does the story of Noah (Genesis 4:1–16) and the account of events leading up to the flood dispel the idea that, left to his own devices, man would produce a better environment to live in?

5. In the early chapters of Genesis, we observe God's judgement. Can you also note his grace and mercy in the event in the Garden of Eden and his dealings with Noah?

6. Read Genesis 12. Abraham knew very little of God.

▷ In this chapter, what demands did God make of him?
▷ What promises were made to him?
▷ What can you learn from the way Abraham reacted?
▷ How do you see God's plan beginning to take shape for the world throughout the ages? (See Hebrews 6:13–20.)
▷ If you were in Abraham's position, having to be prepared to leave your security, home and country, how do you think you would react?

Start some longer-term Bible study, looking at:
(a) God's missionary heart

▷ Exodus 20:4–6.
▷ Numbers 14:21.
▷ Deuteronomy 4:23–24.
▷ Isaiah 6:3; 11:9; 40:5; 42:1–8.
▷ Habakkuk 2:14.

(b) God's missionary promises

▷ Genesis 12:3.
▷ Matthew 28:16–20.
▷ Galatians 3:8.
▷ Isaiah 44:1–5.
▷ Joel 2:28–30.
▷ John 4:14; 10:10; 15:1–11.
▷ Luke 10:1–2.
▷ Revelation 2:10.

4

The Reluctant Mover

As you get to know God better, you realize his ability to perform the unexpected. As soon as you think you have a situation perfectly under control, God comes and surprises you. The boundaries we create in our thinking and by our expectations, are regularly demolished by his power.

If you were to wake up tomorrow morning to the news that Libya had been turned into a smoking ruin following a bombing raid, how would you react?

What would you do if it was made known in your church that the future programme of outreach was to be directed at frequenters of 'The Rat and Corkscrew' public house, the local nightclub, and the National Front? In the back of your mind, would you be concerned that if people from these groups were converted, they might bring unhelpful influences into the church? You could lose your favourite seat to a large skinhead with a Union Jack tatoo on the back of his neck. Would we really want to see the publican, prostitute and political activist converted?

It is very difficult to acknowledge our own prejudices, and where self-interest lies. Would we really prefer to see Colonel Gadaffi punished for his support of terrorism rather than have the opportunity to repent and turn to Christ? The question would become even more pertinent if God were to say to you, 'Go to Libya and preach against it.' Most of us would opt for a Mediterranean cruise, rather than go too near the Middle East.

Jonah faced a similar challenge when God told him to go to the great city of Nineveh (Jonah 1:2). Jonah has often been treated harshly by preachers who underestimate the difficulties he faced. We are all more than capable of doing as Jonah did.

The book of Jonah has been surrounded by controversy because of the supernatural element within it. Those who refuse to entertain the supernatural provision of a great fish, and a giant gourd to protect Jonah from the heat, have to find other explanations. The book has been variously interpreted under the headings of mythology, allegory, commentary, parable and history. The result of the controversy has been neglect, and a failure to appreciate the importance of this book within the Bible, and within God's plan of salvation.

We may have confidence in the book being an historical record of accounts, for the following reasons:

1. There is no hint in the text that the account is merely allegory or a parable.

2. The account describes a definite historical figure who is fully involved in the events.

3. Jewish tradition has accepted the book as history.

4. Christ's references to events in Matthew 12 suggest that he accepted the reliability of the account.[3]

An open-air preacher was once confronted by a devout atheist:

Atheist: Do you really believe that Jonah spent three days and nights in the belly of a fish?

Preacher: I don't know sir, but when I get to heaven I'll ask him.

Atheist: But suppose he isn't in heaven?

Preacher Then you ask him.

Whatever our view on the historicity of the book, our

attention must move to its message, which has many
facets. One is to demonstrate that God cares for those outside Israel. Jonah was a Jew and fiercely patriotic. He was
confident that God was only dealing with his nation and
could not really be interested in the people of Nineveh. He
was sure that what the people required was a good dose of
God's judgement. They had been brutal and godless and
the destruction of their city was the least they deserved.
What concerned Jonah was that if the people did repent,
the God he knew would be merciful and not destroy them.
He knew for himself the kindness of God but could not
bear to think of it being extended.

Israel had been the object of God's special love in order
that they should make it known to others. Jonah may be
seen as a representative of the Jewish people who are
proud of their relationship with God, but unwilling to fulfil
their responsibility to act as a 'light for the Gentiles'
(Isaiah 42:6). In order to maintain their distinctiveness,
they cut themselves off from the other nations, because of
a fear of infiltration by worshippers of other gods. As a
result, the nation thought it had exclusive rights to God
and failed to be a significant missionary force to be
reckoned with.

It was not God's intention that the Jews should be like
the pagan cults in adopting narrow, exclusive attitudes.
From the beginning it had been God's purpose that stran-
gers should have a share in the blessings of salvation.[4]

The years during which Jesus' ministry took place were
marked by a resurgence of missionary activity by the Jews.
Through their belief in one God, their stand against pagan
idolatry and immorality, many people were blessed. The
translation of the Hebrew Old Testament into Greek,
backed by the quality of life of devout Jews, all had their
appeal to Gentiles. Some gave up their heathen practices
and started attending the synagogues. For others it meant
adopting the Jewish religion, following baptism, the
bringing of sacrifice and in the case of men, circumcision.

The possibility was there for non-Jews to be included. When Jesus was speaking in Matthew 23:15, he declared: 'Woe to you ... [who] travel over land and sea to win a single convert, and when he becomes one, you make him twice as much a son of hell as you are.' Jesus' complaint was that the Pharisees were not merely out to make converts, but to make replicas of themselves. In fact, their desire was to create even more zealous, legalistic, hair-splitting, law-keeping Pharisees. It was hoped that the new converts would become fanatical evangelists for their new-found faith. R.G. Tasker comments, 'Those converted, tended to become the perverted.'[5] Such enthusiasm for evangelism was not found too frequently in Israel's history.

Jonah was not a man with a missionary zeal, and he represented a nation that was quite content to be a recipient of God's blessing, without taking responsibility for sharing it. As well as complacency, some would have said, 'How we have suffered at the hands of heathen nations in the past! How many times has our land been invaded and become the battlefield for the great power blocks to the north and south?' Jonah's lack of confidence in God to go with him to Nineveh, reflected the depressed and introverted state of God's people at the time.

This situation has some obvious similarities to the church today. Many are quite content with little growth, as long as there is the hope that God is smiling benevolently on our activities. While we are concerned about our personal needs being met, the church becomes more distant from the general population, and less aware of the needs of the rest of the world. We can build our own religious sub-culture where we sing hymns, worship songs and perform our other worth-while religious activities. More experienced people will initiate us into the particular behaviour patterns of the group we have joined. Some will quickly learn that to be accepted, you require a dark suit or a tambourine, but preferably not both! Once you become part of the 'inner circle', you suddenly realize that all your energy is taken in maintaining what already exists. As time goes by, it becomes harder to speak in a natural way about Christ, because you have become removed from those you are communicating with.

We are largely unaware of the worldwide impact that groups such as the Jehovah's Witnesses and the Mormons are having. The Mormons from Salt Lake City have more missionaries than all the churches in the UK, Canada, Australia and New Zealand put together. They have 24,000 young men on the march today! Each one of those young men is responsible for the baptism of two new converts each year. Each convert, so they estimate, takes 500 hours of door-to-door visitation.[6] A missionary in Indonesia reported a conversation with a leader of the Muslim community, in which he stated that unless the Christian church produced more people suitable for high office in national life, they would soon be replaced by Muslims. Once that happened the Christian influence in the country would decline.

The challenge to our isolation is plain to observe. In 1972, there were 5,300 Protestant missionaries serving overseas. By 1982, the number had decreased to 4,748.[7] While any of us can walk into a Christian bookshop and select from a vast range of Christian literature, there are many countries where a modern version of the Bible is not available. There are still 3,000 languages into which no part of the Bible is translated. It was popular a few years ago, to talk of the near completion of the missionary task. Such talk reflected a loss of confidence and growing insularity in the face of evidence to the contrary. At least one third of the world's population has had no exposure to the claims of Christ. There are 3–4,000 distinct groups of people in the world where there are no believers.[8] It is estimated that the world's population will double in the next forty years. The millions now gathering in the world's cities are among the hardest to reach with the gospel.

While we attempt to come to terms with our 'Jonah complexes', little enthusiasm for evangelism is generated. Once we settle into our cosy little Christian communities, the world outside can seem a hostile and dangerous place. We think that if our fellowship, worship, doctrine, church practice and discipline are all of the highest quality, God will bless us. To our surprise, we find that God is at work in the strangest places. We may find the local Pentecostal Church is suddenly bursting at the seams, and in the High Church there are those who display clear evidence of being Spirit-filled. Once we have failed to find suitable explanations to protect our superior position, we have to acknowledge that God is sovereign, and works where he chooses. Jonah was quite content with God's sphere of activity being exactly where he was.

Running

In Jonah 1:1–2, God moved to shatter Jonah's introspective outlook. God, for his own reasons, had decided that Jonah was the man for this mission. Jonah was not told of any reward for being obedient; he was simply told to go to Nineveh. All kinds of thoughts must have gone through his mind: 'This is ridiculous. Nobody has ever done anything like this before. People will laugh at me. Nineveh is the great city of the day with over half a million people. They are our enemies. For centuries it has been growing in power and influence, and God wants me to go and tell the people to repent. If they are given the opportunity to repent, they might just do that. Then where would we be? Only the Jews could be God's people. We don't really want any of that lot from Nineveh. No thanks!'

God clearly communicated the task to Jonah. He was left in no doubt about the destination and the message he must proclaim. The word of God must be obeyed. It has always taken sacrifices to be involved in missionary activity. Many who went from Britain in the last century never even arrived, having died at sea.

On January 5th, 1956, in the jungles of Ecuador, five young men were killed by Auca Indians. The men had wanted to speak to them of Christ. Before his death one of the young men, Jim Elliot, wrote in his diary, 'He is no fool who gives what he cannot keep in order to gain what he cannot lose.' Life is short. We must not cling tightly to what we will lose. When God's command is clear, it must be obeyed. Jonah was told to go because the task was urgent. Any delay would give time for the doubts to arise and for the wrong direction to be taken.

Jonah, with his strong feelings of national superiority and proud exclusiveness, did start moving—but in the wrong direction. Israel knew that it was to be treated favourably by God, but could not bear to think of that same grace being extended to others.

God's plans could not be stopped. He made alternative arrangements involving some sailors, a storm and a large fish. Jonah was going to have a personal encounter with the all-powerful God.

Circumstances favoured Jonah's plan to escape to Tarshish, a place where he thought God might leave him alone. A ship was available to transport him away from the troubles he encountered in his own land. His speed of departure indicated the strength of desire to flee.

The availability of a ready escape route can be an attractive option when God says we must do something we would rather not do. Departure from God involves a departure from his intimate love and protection. We are at peace when we do as God commands, but when we turn away from him, the consequences are serious. There are many directed by God to go as his representatives into different situations, both at home and abroad, who never arrive. Other attractions arise in their thinking and the eventual destination is not the one originally intended. Justification will have to be found, to create a partial peace of mind, but there is little fruitfulness. God does not usually intervene to halt our self-motivated actions, but the account of Jonah is a warning that he can.

'The Lord sent a great wind on the sea' (Jonah 1:4). God's first action to affect the situation, was to send a storm. God who created the forces of nature, now exercised his control over them. The wind began to blow and the sea became more turbulent. God's anger was made known and Jonah was going to find that disobedience has consequences. There are times when God causes the wind to blow in our direction. It may be to warn us or show us there is something we must do, and we stubbornly refuse.

The consequences for the ship were serious. It threatened to break up. There had been many previous occasions when the ship had been caught in bad weather, but never as seriously as the day Jonah was on board. The experienced sailors had never seen anything like this before, and were afraid. Their fear drove them to pray. In the face of great danger, and the awareness that they could do nothing themselves to help the situation, they sought help from their gods. On calm days, it would have been easy to forget their gods, but now there were problems and they cried out for help. Their concern was so great that Jonah was raised from sleep and told to call on his God.

Sleeping

Jonah must have felt rebuked by the captain who woke him up. While others are in danger, it is no time to take your ease. Everything that can be done must be done. The prophet Amos warned: 'Woe to you who are complacent in Zion' (Amos 6:1). There could be no resting for Jonah while a message from God had to be conveyed to Nineveh. His refusal was putting other lives in jeopardy. There can be no complacency in our day when faced by the masses who do not know Christ. Many of our churches have become like holiday camps where we enjoy ourselves, rather than bases from which to engage in spiritual warfare. Jonah was being exhorted by a man who did not have faith in his god. He may have had some knowledge of the power and reputation of Jonah's God and felt he could help.

When one of God's people becomes disobedient, the consequences affect many others. It is very sobering to be rebuked by a non-Christian for being in a place that displeases God, or for failing to be concerned for the welfare of others. Once Jonah opened his eyes and saw the storm, he must have been aware of God's displeasure, but worse than the captain's rebuke was to come. They set out to find the source of the problem.

Up until that point, Jonah had kept his true identity secret. Like many, he did not want to reveal his identity. He didn't want anyone to realize that he was a Hebrew, part of a despised minority. God's people cannot hide, no matter how hard they try. In our current attempts to identify and appear 'relevant', it is easy to lose our distinctiveness. We may want to show non-Christians that we are just 'ordinary people' in order to build a relationship with them. In our attempts to relate to people, we may start thinking that the message needs some minor adjustments to make it more acceptable. Subjects like sin, death and judgement produce a negative emotional response, so it may be better not to include them!

The sailors arranged for lots to be cast in order to find out who was responsible for the storm. God overruled the casting of the lot and Jonah was revealed as the source of the problem. He was then subjected to a fierce interrogation: 'Who is responsible for making all this trouble for us? What do you do? Where do you come from? What is your country?' (Jonah 1:8). When he boarded the ship, Jonah thought he was escaping trouble, but now the full consequences of his disobedience were coming to light. It is no good attempting to conceal our true identity. The truth will come out. Soon the sailors made the connection between Jonah's disobedience to God and their own predicament. Jonah's sin was disclosed. Sin frequently tries to deceive with secrecy, but with little success. As a result of the questioning, Jonah confessed his faith without any qualifications.

Confessing

Jonah declared that he was a Hebrew; a name used of Abraham's descendants and indicating a position of privilege. He was one of God's special people and therefore his sins had the most severe consequences. Jonah also identified himself as a worshipper of the Lord, Yahweh. His religion was more than nationalistic, it was personal. The God he worshipped was not like the sailors' God, who was merely a great power somewhere in the universe. As a Hebrew, Jonah had a particular relationship with Yahweh, which was not shared with the sailors. There are many who claim to believe in some God who exists somewhere, but is not in any way personal. People are saying that in all religions we worship the same God—we just call him by different names. To declare with Peter, 'Salvation is found in no-one else, for there is no other name under heaven given to men by which we must be saved' (Acts 4:12), is to be labelled intolerant and exclusive. Christianity declares that there is no other route to the Father except through Christ (John 14:6). The teaching of theologians who stress we should emphasize the common characteristics of religions, has had a subtle influence on our thinking and missionary zeal. If the early Christian missionaries had accepted these views, the foundations they laid for the rapid Christian growth in Third World countries would never have been established. The decline in Christian influence within Eastern Europe and the West is disturbing, but the growth in other areas is most exciting. The following figures giving the proportion of all Christians as a percentage of the populations, illustrates the trends:[9]

	1900	1970	1980	1985
The West and Europe	99%	64%	50%	34%
The Third World	1%	36%	50%	66%

Has the church in the Western World lost its confidence in the cutting edge of the gospel? Is it possible that our brothers and sisters in the Third World are more ready to take God at his word and act upon it? Have we been asleep in the back of the boat for fear that we might be identified too closely as God's people?

Jonah could not keep his true identity concealed any longer. He made a clear confession that he worshipped the one and only God, the Maker and Sustainer of the universe, who is the Guide and Saviour of all men. Having realized there was no escaping from such a God, he disclosed information that would lay himself open to contempt and possibly death. He held nothing back, and said, 'Pick me up and throw me into the sea' (Jonah 1:12). Confession is always difficult because we like to think we are always right. Jonah recognized that it was his disobedience that led to God's displeasure, and that the only hope for the rest of the crew was to drop him overboard.

The sailors, on hearing Jonah's confession, were even more afraid. Not this time of the wind and waves, but of the power of Jonah's God. They were beginning to realize that there was no comparison between their gods and Jehovah. Jonah's God was not made in their imaginations, but was real. It was obvious that Jehovah was angry and they were afraid. In our late twentieth-century brand of Christianity, it is not very often people think that God is to be feared. He is much too loving to cause us to fear him. Fear can produce positive as well as negative reactions. The little boy who attempted to fly through a glass window, is now afraid of going too close to glass. Such a fear results in a healthy respect. To know what it is to fear God, is most important.

Around us there are people who are afraid of the dark,

or maybe even cats. Others fear being rejected and unloved. But how many fear God? The sailors encountered God as he really is and because of their sin, they were afraid. Jonah realized he could not flee from God, and was prepared to take the consequences of his actions. Both Jonah and the sailors realized that Jehovah God was not to be taken so lightly. God, in his love, must punish sin.

When there are people who truly fear God, and as a result live authentic Christian lives, others will sit up and take note. If Christians think that God does not notice or mind our minor sins, we will lose our credibility with unbelievers. They will start thinking that sin does not really matter and if Christians behave as if there is no God to be reckoned with, why shouldn't they? Our lives must support the message we proclaim. Without Christians living the lives that support and confirm the message, people will not listen to us. What the sailors saw and heard in Jonah's confession, convinced them that some action was necessary. The last resort would be to throw him overboard, but before that they tried their best to row back to the land.

The action of the sailors is highly commendable. By their own actions they sought to remedy the situation. This is man's natural reaction to any crisis, but despite the hard physical effort, the storm grew worse. Any self-effort to appease God's wrath will ultimately fail. It is not possible to gain God's approval for what we do by ourselves. The more those men strove to save the situation, the more powerless they became. Their energy was sapped by the effort, and the only solution was for one life to be sacrificed in order for the others to be saved.

It was only with the utmost reluctance, and with a prayer to Jonah's God for pardon, that they agreed to drop Jonah over the side. Their urgent prayer (Jonah 1:14) indicated that through the storm and Jonah's confession, they had transferred their allegiance from their idols to Jehovah. They had been able to make the initial connections between the events in the boat and the power of God. Their confession, 'You, Lord, have done as you pleased,' is remarkable, as it takes many of us years to agree that this is so. All events, however unpleasant, can be traced to God's sovereign will if we make the connections. Behind the events, the hand of God was moving.

Jonah could claim no credit for the conversion of the sailors. He was in the process of rediscovering God for himself, following his disobedience. God can use an obedient or disobedient follower to accomplish his purposes. This is no excuse for spiritual laxity, but there is cause to rejoice as we observe God's activity. The sailors saw far beyond the man Jonah, and encountered God himself. As we know our weakness and tendency to sin, it becomes even more amazing that God can work through people like us. Praise God that he does!

Jonah, on listening to the sailors' sincere prayer, must have wondered why he had been so reluctant to go to Nineveh. Surely if these sailors who had worshipped multi-coloured gods could call out to Jehovah, the people of Nineveh could have done so. As we face the enormous task of reaching people of other religions for God, never let us think the task is impossible. With God's resources in operation, no person can be put in the 'no hopers' category. These men had been prepared by God for the encounter with his reluctant servant. The same God today is preparing people among the so far unreached peoples on earth. Often through events that at first seem disastrous, God is calling a people to himself. The Russian invasion of Afghanistan has led to new opportunities for Christianity to take root in the country. Under previous regimes, the few who responded to the gospel were persecuted and some were killed. The situation is not easy today, but there are more opportunities than ever before. Who would have thought that the resurgence of militant Islam in Iran would lead to many Muslims becoming disenchanted with Islam? The small groups of Christians have been drawn closer together, and are now seeing a higher level of response to their evangelistic activities than ever before. God moves in mysterious ways, his wonders to perform!

The sailors came to the conclusion that Jonah must leave the boat, so he was despatched with prayer to Jehovah. So complete was the change in these men that they prayed, offered sacrifices and made vows (Jonah 1:16). When anyone has real dealings with the true and living God, they cannot be the same again. The God they now know is not some depressed deity waiting for people to recognize him and come to him. They are not of the opinion that in the face of several options this is the right one. Like all people who really know the God of the Bible, they realize there are no favours they can do for God. God is the One who does everything for us.

Sinking

Jonah was prepared to be the sacrifice that would lead to the calming of the troubled seas. The sailors must have thought they were condemning him to a watery grave, but God, in his providence, had other plans. God moved again, this time to provide the great fish. God is never caught unprepared. He was not unaware of the consequences of the fall, and Jesus was always ready to act as Redeemer. When it comes to the conversion of anyone today, God in his goodness and grace has been preparing for that day. In the same way that God could cause the storm to rise and fall, he was able to find a fish of suitable proportions to house Jonah for three days. God's purpose was still that Jonah should go to Nineveh, so he made the necessary arrangements.

Praying

As soon as Jonah was secure within the belly of the great

fish, he cried out to God from what he regarded as hell. He was deeply distressed at being far away from God's presence. This led him to cry to God for help (Jonah 2:2–4) and finally to acknowledge that 'salvation comes from the Lord' (Jonah 2:9). Having been through all that Jonah had, we might say in the circumstances that this was a reasonable conclusion to come to. Both the salvation of his soul, and the physical salvation required to remove him from the fish, could only be arranged by God. Nobody could say that his salvation was due to his temperament, or pressure from an evangelist, or anything else. We cannot find any evidence that Jonah contributed anything to his salvation. It was not part of his action and part of God's action. It could have only been God's action. Jonah's salvation was complete when the fish decided that three days of discomfort to the digestive system was sufficient, and deposited Jonah on dry land. He was not left with a long swim—the rescue was complete.

Jonah had come to appreciate many things from the time he first set foot in the boat. He had learned something vital in his dealings with the sailors. Previously he had thought of salvation in narrow nationalistic terms. To his surprise, God had used the storm to reveal himself to a bunch of heathen sailors. Jonah did not really think this was possible. Now his horizons were broadening, but at this stage he must have felt a great failure. Jonah must have wondered with his track record of disasters in evangelism if he could be of any use again. Following his attempt to get away from God and the trouble he had caused to the sailors, he might well have thought dying in the belly of the fish a reasonably attractive proposition.

If we abuse the confidence of the people we work for, and cause them trouble, they will seldom forgive and allow us another opportunity. God is different. He freely forgives, following repentance, and leads us into a life of usefulness again. It would have been quite reasonable for God to feel that having failed once, Jonah was going to fail again and was therefore not to be trusted any more. God is a specialist in making use of those who have failed and feel they have let others down. Abraham, David and Simon Peter are some examples. Jonah knew so much more about his God at this stage and was ready for a second commissioning.

Preaching

The word of the Lord came a second time to Jonah: 'Go to the great city of Nineveh and proclaim to it the message I give you' (Jonah 3:1–2).

God was in no way obliged to come a second time to Jonah, but his servant had been punished and corrected enough, and the message still had to be proclaimed in Nineveh. God's plans still had to be accomplished. Jonah's disobedience meant a delay in the city-dwellers hearing God's voice, but nothing was going to stop them having the opportunity.

God gives all his people tasks to accomplish, and expects them to do it. Any delays are signs of lack of trust. We must be willing and prepared for the time when God says 'go'. His simple and clear word must be heard and obeyed. Jonah was not expected to rely on any natural skills of communication, because the promise was that the message to proclaim would be given to him. The words he was to convey were from God himself. Jonah was not at liberty to subtract anything. He was not to attempt to make it easier for the people to accept. The message was going to be unwelcome, but it had to be delivered.

We have no liberty today to reinterpret God's message so that people may find it more palatable. The great truths of the Bible are unchanging and must be proclaimed faithfully—no matter how people may react. The message of man's sin and his disobedience will always be unpopular and cause people to be offended. Those who fail to proclaim the truth, as found in Scripture, are warned that the preaching of another gospel will lead to eternal condemnation (Galatians 1:8).

God meant it when he first said 'go' to Jonah. He has always had the needs of those who do not know him close to his heart. Jonah, on hearing the call for the second time, promptly obeyed. Whereas he had been reluctant, now he was responsive. He neither delayed nor stopped on the way to Nineveh. On arrival, he had the great task of proclaiming God's message to the people. There was a note of urgency about his preaching: 'Forty more days and Nineveh will be destroyed' (Jonah 3:4).

Urgent preaching that proclaimed God's message was the means chosen to reach the city-dwellers. At a time when we may be inclined to place emphasis on anything but preaching, we need to remember that this is God's appointed way. We may seek to ensure that our music is improved, or that our drama group is functioning effectively, but forget that preaching is vital. 'God was pleased through the foolishness of what was preached to save those who believe' (1 Corinthians 1:21).

Jonah knew that he had a message from God, and with boldness proclaimed it. When God is about to work in a dramatic way, it will be accompanied by a resurgence of authentic preaching. The proclamation of God's truth is not just to be done by people standing in pulpits. It is to be done day by day as God's followers make known God's truth. When the opportunity arises, we all have a responsibility to tell clearly God's truth.

Jonah's message was brief, and could be understood by all. He did not use clever oratory, but the words struck at the consciences of the people, and there was a tremendous response. The citizens of Nineveh knew what it was to face the possibility of being overthrown from within or without. From within the city could have come a conspiracy or revolt. They could have earthquakes or floods. There was always the threat of nations they had oppressed coming to seek revenge. Whatever the reason, the message of God convicted the people of their guilt, and they knew that if they were destroyed, they would receive only what they deserved. God's judgement is always just.

Repenting

The extent of the repentance is seen by its effect on the King, the people and even the animals in the area (Jonah 3:7). The word hit home to the King, who would have had supreme authority over all matters. For the King to repent in such a dramatic way would have had a tremendous effect on the people. All bowed in humiliation before the God who was angry with them. Their repentance was not just in word, it was followed by clear evidence of its reality. Both people and animals were to fast in order to call urgently on God. The putting on of sackcloth was to show visibly that they were really sorry for their sins. A new way was about to open up to the people as they cried with all their might, not to the idols they had previously worshipped, but to the true God who alone could help.

Jonah's message contained no hope of mercy. The only theme was one of judgement. A sense of hope existed in the people who prayed: 'Who knows? God may relent' (Jonah 3:9). Although they had limited knowledge of God, the only possibility of them having any future was if God would hold back from the action he had threatened. God is always gracious, if people will genuinely turn to him. The whole city was preserved and no one was killed.

The events in Nineveh show us the capacity of people outside Israel to repent and turn to God. Jonah's initial fear that this would happen because of God's graciousness actually materialized. There was a clear contrast between Jonah's grudging spirit and the responsiveness of first the sailors, and then the city of Nineveh. As a Jew, Jonah was confident of God's mercy, but the others could not take it for granted and could only repent and plead more earnestly for forgiveness. God granted forgiveness, and clearly illustrated his concern for all men, regardless of their religious background. Sincere repentance will always be met by forgiveness.

Mission accomplished! The visit of Jonah to Ninevah was a tremendous success. If it had happened today, the top investigative reporters of a news-hungry media would have been despatched to provide an 'in-depth analysis'.

But Jonah was far from pleased by God's display of mercy. He was so angry, that given half a chance he would have demolished the city all by himself.

Grumbling

Jonah slipped out of the city, and poured out his wrath to God. 'I told you so, didn't I? You sent me to tell Nineveh it would be reduced to a pile of rubble. Now you are not going to lift a finger to give them what they deserve. The people are wicked and should be punished. I'm fed up. If you aren't going to kill them, I wish you would kill me.'

Jonah and Israel are shown here in the worst possible light. They were quite content to receive God's mercy, but could not bear it being given to others. His confession, 'I knew that you are a gracious and compassionate God, slow to anger and abounding in love, a God who relents from sending calamity' (Jonah 4:2), was only to be understood in narrow nationalistic terms. He loved his own people more than the Ninevites, and God's grace to them did not please him.

Christians today often have the same spirit, where they idolize their own church, denomination or particular grouping. Jonah's sin is not uncommon today. We can be just as nationalistic and narrow minded, to the detriment of local and worldwide evangelism. When other groups, very different from our own, are blessed by God, we have a tendency to find fault with their methods and the people involved.

Jonah needed to be made aware that God breaks

through the barriers that we can erect. He settled down despite the intense heat, to wait forty days, in the hope that Nineveh would be destroyed. God caused a plant to grow which was large enough to shelter the prophet from the sun's heat. Jonah was very happy about the provision of the vine. The next day, before the sun was peeping over the horizon, a worm came and started gnawing its way through the vine, and it withered. It turned out to be a hot day and God was about to reveal the folly of Jonah's attitude. A scorching east wind brought Jonah to the point of desperation. He had had enough; he was tired and depressed. He would rather have died. God asked Jonah: '"Do you have a right to be angry about the vine?" "I do," he said' (Jonah 4:9).

God went on to explain that Jonah was able to feel sympathy for the gourd and pity for himself. Could he find it in himself to understand how God feels pity for the city of Nineveh with its 120,000 plus small children? If Jonah could feel so upset about the loss of the vine, to whose existence he had contributed nothing, was not God permitted to show concern for those in Nineveh whom he had created? God's compassion extends to all. He longs for people to repent and turn to him.

Jonah was left speechless. If the great fish had still been around, he might gladly have been swallowed up. Having been rebuked, Jonah must have recorded, at a later date, the events for the Jewish people and those reading today, to benefit from his experience. The book concludes with visions of God's all-embracing love. It is the one completely missionary book in the Old Testament. What at first reading appears to be a simple story, has much more to teach us. It powerfully illustrates:

1. *God's concern for unbelieving nations.* The object of God's special love is Israel, but he is not unconcerned for others. His heart is one of compassion and it responds to repentance.

2. *The responsibility given by God to those who are*

unaware of him. The Ninevites were clearly responsible for their wickedness and would be judged for it. Their repentance indicated that they knew they were morally wrong. They were capable of being judged on the basis of the light from God that they did possess (Romans 2:12–16).

People today, who know nothing of Christ, are in the same position. If a few more Jonahs leave the confines of home and the security of church and walk into a situation where God is at work, thousands could respond. God is not unresponsive to the needs of the unbeliever. He prepares his messengers and says to them 'go'. Although Jonah was unwilling, God did not desert the runaway because he disobeyed the command. He disciplined him and gave him another opportunity. The 'reluctant mover' eventually found himself in the right place.

When God says 'go', we must not say 'no'.

THINK IT THROUGH

1. Imagine your church is invaded on successive Sundays by a dozen skinheads, a group of rowdy publicans and a crowd of students from overseas. How would you react? Would your reactions help or hinder these people?

2. Are there signs in Jonah 3 and 4 that Jonah had learnt anything from his earlier experience? Was he in any sense a changed man?

3. Relate the message of Jonah to Peter's vision in Acts 10. What similarities do you see?

4. In what ways do you think Jonah's reluctance is illustrative of current attitudes to mission?

5. What are some of the marks of introspection in your church? What steps are required to turn an ingrown church outwards?

6. How does your church rate when it comes to being involved in mission? Use these questions and comments

to promote reaction and discussion.

▷ When it comes to missionary events, everyone is: Excited / Interested / Not too keen / Arranges to be away.

▷ The majority of church finance goes to: Maintaining the work at home / Supporting God's work elsewhere.

▷ Missionary events are: A regular part of the church programme / Occasional events / Rare occurrences

▷ Our church has a Missionary Council / Missionary Activists group that acts as a catalyst to encourage missionary activity. They set goals and review them annually.

▷ The leadership of the church should actively be seeking out people who may become missionaries.

▷ The membership of the church should actively encourage their leaders to make visits to overseas missionary situations.

▷ The local church should provide its own programme in basic Christian service.

▷ Discuss together how your church could become more actively involved in mission. What opportunities are available locally to contact minority groups?

5

God's Greatest Move

The growth of atheism, and the resurgence of Islam, pose a real challenge to a comfortable and complacent Western church. Many are totally committed to their cause and are fanatical in their desire that others should share their beliefs. 'Philosophers,' wrote Karl Marx, 'have only interpreted the world differently; the point is, however, to change it.' One young South American communist wrote: 'We communists have a high casualty rate. We're the ones who get shot and hung and lynched and jailed and slandered and fired from our jobs, and in every other way made as uncomfortable as possible. We have a philosophy of life that no amount of money can buy. We have a cause to fight for, a definite purpose in life. We *are* fanatics. Our lives are dominated by one great overshadowing factor—the struggle for world Communism.'

A young man fired with that commitment is going to influence others. Those who achieve anything in life must have clear objectives in view, coupled with a fierce determination.

We have observed, in the Old Testament, God's desire to have a people for himself—Israel. He is also interested in making himself known to all people. All the forward pointers in the Old Testament meet when we encounter Jesus Christ. In his coming, Jesus discloses more of God's great desire to communicate with those he created.

The motivation of Jesus

Jesus did not come in pursuit of his own interests or prestige, but with the specific desire to please his Father: 'For I always do what pleases him' (John 8:29). He came not only to represent his Father, but to make visible what had been previously unseen; namely God himself. This was the 'Light of the world' which the world had been waiting for. Through his actions, Jesus clearly demonstrated what God is like. God is the One who shines his light in our direction.

The mission of Jesus

Jesus was continually looking out for people. The account given in Luke 19 gives clear evidence of his outgoing nature. Jericho was a city famous for its palm trees and rose gardens. It had a pleasant climate where you could enjoy the delights of the theatre or the grand palace. You could mingle with the wealthy and enjoy the tree-lined streets. Modern-day travel agents would probably compare Jericho with a town like Bath or Cheltenham.

The tranquillity of the city had been rather spoilt, because the occupying Roman army needed to tax people heavily. Keeping soldiers in the land, and paying for the luxurious lifestyle of some back in Rome, was an expensive business. The local tax collectors were not highly paid by the Romans, but had a certain liberty to overcharge the locals and pocket the excess.

Zacchaeus had responsibility as the chief tax collector for one of the three tax districts in Palestine. People have never been keen on paying tax, especially when the money is going to a foreign, heathen power. Zacchaeus would have been regarded as a collaborator, and was a very unpopular man. Despite his ability, affluence and position in life, Zacchaeus was a profoundly dissatisfied individual. Through his circumstances, God had been preparing him for an encounter with Jesus. The encounter he had with Jesus is another excellent example of the sovereignty of God in action and man's responsibility.

Jesus was on his final journey to Jerusalem, where he was to face death. While he was concentrating on what was to come, Jesus quite deliberately took time out to find Zacchaeus. This was to be the last known convert of Christ before the events of the cross, and therefore assumes special significance.

Zacchaeus could have remained where he was and kept away from Jesus. Instead he had a real desire to at least catch a glimpse of the man who was causing such a commotion in Jericho. Knowing the likely route that Jesus would take, he hitched up his robes and started moving. Have you ever seen an eminent person run? It was Aristotle who said, 'Great men never run.' What would the British press make of the Chancellor of the Exchequer, dressed in his best pinstripe suit, briefcase in one hand and brolly in the other, dashing from Downing Street to a tree in Regents Park, because he wanted to see Jesus?

The sycamore tree Zacchaeus climbed was not of the tall and erect variety found in Britain. It had a short trunk and its spreading branches might have had a diameter of up to seventy feet. On a hot sunny day, it would have provided excellent shade, and on this occasion, gave Zacchaeus a good vantage point from which to observe Jesus. To the surprise of the little tax collector, Jesus stopped under his tree and said, 'Zacchaeus, come down immediately. I must stay at your house today' (Luke 19:5).

When Jesus is looking for someone, it does not matter whether they are in a crowd or up a tree. He called to the man by name and everyone would have noted the authority with which he spoke. The matter he wanted to speak to

Zacchaeus about was urgent and needed to be settled quickly.

We will not find any other instances in the gospels, of Jesus volunteering his company in this way. Zacchaeus was a very special man chosen to demonstrate Christ's concern for the needy and outcasts in society. There was an obvious willingness on his part to speak with Jesus. Christ does not go where he is not welcome. He told the seventy-two disciples in Luke 10 to be prepared to move on if they were not well received. For Zacchaeus, the thought of Jesus coming to his household was an exciting one and they went off together. You can imagine the crowd wondering: 'Did you see Jesus walking down the street with Zacchaeus?'

'He's at it again! Jesus is with one of the worst sinners in the whole community.'

'Do you remember that tax collector Matthew? He's one of Jesus' disciples. Now Zacchaeus. What's the world coming to?'

'This situation has got completely out of hand. We must put a stop to it.'

Luke records that 'all the people saw this and began to mutter' (Luke 19:7). Their failure to understand the purpose of Jesus' mission, or to have compassion on Zacchaeus, is very evident. Following the private meeting with Jesus, which must have included genuine repentance, Zacchaeus made sure that all wrongs were put right. Many in Jericho must have been surprised by the radical transformation in their leading tax official. They would also have been financially better off following the visit of Jesus to their town.

Zacchaeus is one man who was told clearly what the mission of Jesus is: 'For the Son of Man came to seek and to save what was lost' (Luke 19:10). A more concise definition of the purposes of Christ's coming would be hard to find. It only took fourteen words. It didn't matter if it was a sinful woman from Samaria, a demon possessed

man, or an untouchable leper, they were all capable of
being found by Jesus.

The ministry of Jesus

God did not shout at us from the heavens. He didn't wait
until the age of mass communications to beam his message, via a satellite, around the globe. He chose to do
something far more simple. To disclose to the world his
nature, he became one of us.

All the status and glory of heaven was exchanged for a
life of complete identification with us. He did not proclaim his love from a safe and respectable distance, but
became totally involved with us. Christ is our example of
how to reach out of our nice, comfortable circle of Christian friends to others in need. Jesus was remarkably open
with people. Although constantly in the public eye, he
was not afraid to disclose his feelings. He didn't mind
being seen weeping at the death of a friend, Lazarus, or
experiencing the emotional pain at Gethsemane. We find
him asking for support from others and allowing women
such as Mary Magdalene to minister to him. Jesus was not
the son of some far-off deity who disliked any human contact. He was not a preacher, happier in the pulpit than
talking to people. Jesus could be enjoyable company at a
party or wedding. He didn't spend all his time issuing
orders, but went and met people face to face.

Those whom Jesus encountered thought a religious
man was an unapproachable man. To their surprise, Jesus
established meaningful contact with people very quickly.
His openness and integrity drew people around him.
Some would want to touch him physically, others to have
their children taken in his arms. Throughout his ministry,
Jesus demonstrated that what really mattered was his
Father and people.

Jesus himself described the purpose of his ministry: 'The
Son of Man did not come to be served, but to serve, and to

give his life as a ransom for many' (Matthew 20:28). John records: 'He now showed them the full extent of his love' (John 13:1), by taking water and a towel and washing the dirty feet of his disciples. Jesus was not afraid to get his hands dirty. In doing so he took the humble position of the servant, not of the dynamic, influential leader we might expect today. His attitudes and actions set his disciples, then and now, an example of what Christian ministry is all about: service. This service included the care of people's bodies as well as their souls. He would confront sickness and may be described as the first medical missionary. In a world where the weak were often despised and given no support, Jesus shines as the example of kindness. For Jesus, serving others was not an occasional activity at special times, but the driving force in his life.

When faced with apparently impossible situations or people, Jesus always saw the potential for what they could become. No matter how low someone's personal circumstances had sunk, there was always hope. He had a profound hatred for those who felt they had such personal security that they were entitled to look down on others. Some of his most severe words were reserved for those who claimed an exclusive right to the mercy of God, while denying it to others.

Jesus knew that our lives are greatly enriched by service and self-denial. Not only did he demonstrate this personally, but spoke of it frequently. The willingness to deny self and do some cross-carrying was to be the mark of a disciple (Matthew 16:24–26). Rather than consider the outcast and the rejected as people to be ignored, they are there to be helped. In the parable of the sheep and goats in Matthew 25:31–46, Jesus is saying that the test to be applied at the Day of Judgement is not: do you have your doctrine wrapped in a neat parcel? but: how did you serve others? Jesus said, 'Whatever you did for one of the least of these brothers of mine, you did for me' (Matthew 25:40).

The loving heart of God resulted in total self-giving

being demonstrated by Jesus Christ. It was to reveal the
love of God that he came. He set an example for his disciples in all ages and circumstances. Agape love has the
ability to break down the most firmly erected barriers.
This love is the deep root from which the service of Jesus
sprang. It could not be manufactured, but could only
result from the divine love of God.

If you have the opportunity to hear people pray, you
quickly realize what really occupies their minds. I did hear
of one missionary prayer meeting where someone prayed
for all the people in the uninhabited parts of the world.
This possibly suggested there was not much going on in his
mind.

Those who observed the prayer life of Jesus had an
excellent opportunity to discover what really moved him.
Prayer was the prevailing habit of Christ's life. Despite all
the 'people pressure' he was under, and that his main
ministry was to be crammed into three short years, Jesus
made time to pray. For such a demanding ministry Jesus
knew it was essential to keep in constant contact with his
Father. To face the challenges, a firm resolve was necessary. The limited number of recorded prayers demonstrate Jesus' love and the outgoing nature of God.

Jesus prayed for other people

Although faced with enormous personal pressures, Jesus
prayed for Simon Peter who was going to face a time of
real testing from Satan: 'But I have prayed for you, Simon,
that your faith may not fail' (Luke 22:32). The prayer on
the cross that God will forgive his enemies is quite remarkable in the circumstances (Luke 23:34). In the great high-
priestly prayer of John 17, Jesus is to be found praying for
his immediate disciples and those who will succeed them in
the future generations. In this prayer, there is a vision of
what is to come. He sees the growing results throughout
the world following his great self-sacrifice on the cross.

The disciples will have to make their sacrifices, but their influence will grow and the gospel will spread. There will be one universal body transcending all barriers: his church.

Jesus prays for the success of missionary activity

We know that Jesus would never encourage his followers to pray for something for which he had not prayed himself. When Jesus said, 'Ask the Lord of the harvest, therefore, to send out workers into his harvest field' (Matthew 9:38), we get a glimpse of his desire that others should experience God's love. Jesus expressed this desire following his observations of the crowd who were harassed and helpless. The needs of the people were enormous, yet they had nobody reliable to turn towards for help. In what we call the 'Lord's Prayer' in Matthew 6:9–13, we note the prominent position of the phrase 'Your kingdom come'. We are told to pray first for God's rule and authority to be established, before we ask anything for ourselves. A willingness to pray for God's kingdom to be established, without being personally prepared to be the answer to that prayer, is hypocritical. Prayers that lack the element of intercession for others may quickly become self-centred. This was not the pattern Jesus set for us in prayer.

Following the return of the seventy-two disciples sent out on their evangelistic programmes, Jesus is found praising God: 'I praise you, Father, Lord of heaven and earth, because you have hidden these things from the wise and learned, and revealed them to little children' (Luke 10:21). His heart was full of gratitude to his Father that so many in the surrounding villages were experiencing the power of God. Ordinary people had seen demonic influences overcome and knew that the 'kingdom of God [was] near' (Luke 10:11). As the joyful disciples told each other of God's activity, Jesus gave an indication of the final and complete victory that was to come: 'I saw Satan fall like lightning

from heaven' (Luke 10:18). Before that could happen, the
journey to Jerusalem and the cross had to be faced.

The mediation of Jesus

The cross was the culmination of Christ's ministry. This
was the supreme demonstration of God's outgoing nature.
His love led him to the extreme position of death on a
Roman cross, at the hands of evil men. Jesus experienced
a spiritual pressure, of which we can have little understanding. He had faced the agony of Gethsemane, which
was only the crowning point of his realization that death
awaited him. Jesus, who was fully aware of the Old Testament, knew the prophecies relating to the Suffering Servant in Isaiah. He was not the Messiah of popular expecta-
tion, but the Servant King. The cross with all its terror was
the only means of redemption and he was to be the sin
offering. Through his death, life would come to others.
The iron grip of sin that held all men, was finally to be broken and people could go free.

Paul uses four words in Romans 5:6–10, to diagnose our
fundamental problems before a Holy God. He says that
we are:

(a) Powerless (verse 6). The Greek word here is used to
describe someone who is sick, feeble or deprived of strength
because of disease. If you can remember the last time one of
those dreaded flu bugs took up residence in your system,
you will recall feeling totally limp and unable to do anything to help yourself. This same thought, of being totally
helpless to alter your spiritual state, is what Paul is
describing. It is like the experienced climber being caught
in an unexpected storm while near the top of a mountain.
The cold and darkness sap his energy to the point where he
can make no further progress. Being well trained in mountain survival techniques, this climber knows that the most
sensible thing to do is to stay where he is until rescued.

With God, we are powerless to rescue ourselves. The

more we try, the more frustrated we become and only demonstrate the fact that we are powerless. We are 'dead in our transgressions and sins' (Ephesians 2:1). Dead men do not have the power to live, unless it is given to them by one who is alive. We will only be able to know God's power when we are persuaded we have none of our own.

(b) Ungodly (verse 6). If someone breaks into an art gallery and starts slashing a great masterpiece with a knife, it will only take seconds for him to destroy what has been carefully created. Should he then take from his pocket an aerosol can and spray graffiti all over the remaining pieces, his destruction would be complete. The picture restorers would then face years of painstaking work to restore the painting to its near original condition. Satan has cut and spoiled all that God has created. No amount of matching up the pieces will return us to our original condition. To be 'ungodly' simply means not to be like God.

(c) Sinners (verse 8). One day, someone may invent an electric device that could be placed inside the brain. It would record and play back all our thoughts, words and actions. In our retirement, it would be possible to project onto a screen all that had taken place in our life. The horror that would unfold before us would be too much for us to cope with. We don't have to be told that sin affects us and everyone else. We know we don't grow to be sinners; we are like it naturally. Sin is the dominant force in our lives. Our tendency is always to sin. As we observe the history of the human race, we note that it is a chronicle of wickedness. When a tendency to sin goes unchecked by laws in society, it is not long before any sign of civilization totally breaks down. Dr Henry Kissinger said, 'I think of myself as an historian more than a statesman. As an historian you have to be conscious of the fact that every civilization that has ever existed has ultimately failed. As an historian, one has to live with a sense of the inevitability of tragedy.'

Sin takes and keeps us from God. We see no beauty in Jesus. It sets us outside of his intimate love.

(d) Enemies (verse 10). This is a strong word indicating an active hostility. We are not by nature indifferent to God, but actively against his ways. Because we prefer to follow the ruling tendency of sin, we cannot tolerate absolute rule and authority.

Being described as powerless, ungodly sinners and God's enemies, is not a diagnosis we would choose for ourselves. We are trapped, but thankfully God has provided a solution.

Romans 5:6—'Christ died for the ungodly.'

Romans 5:8—'While we were still sinners, Christ died for us.'

Romans 5:10—'When we were enemies, we were reconciled to him through the death of his Son.'

God's planning has not been haphazard or purely instinctive. Our love is often impulsive and fluctuates according to circumstances. The love of God finds no real comparison with human love. God does not merely possess or exhibit love; his essence is love. All of his activities arise from the fact that he is love. The New Testament writers found no available word adequate to express God's love, so started using the word 'agape'. It was used of a quality of love which longed to give rather than receive. Regardless of the quality of the object, it would still give. We do not possess a love for God that would prompt us to love him. 'We love because he first loved us' (1 John 4:19).

God's great love for helpless, ungodly sinners was to be most powerfully demonstrated in the death of Christ. The love of God was not exhibited by sending a theological statement on the nature of substitutionary atonement. God did not send an angel or a prophet, which we would have been most grateful for, but sent his Son. Nobody can be saved through the life, teaching, miracles or example of Jesus, but only through his death. His body would be offered as a sacrifice for sin. The soul of Jesus would know what it was to be separated from the intimacy of contact with the Father. It was for our sins that Christ died.

The Bible gives us only a small glimpse of the spiritual anguish that Christ went through on the cross. This was God's great act of identification with those who are spiritually dead. John Stott writes: 'No theology is genuinely Christian which does not arise from and focus on the cross.'[10] Christ has done all that is necessary to restore what was ruined by sin. He does not glibly ask or plead with people to accept what he has done for them. A more adequate response to the realization of our sin and the significance of Christ's death, is to call on him to have mercy and accept us.

The fact of the cross has far-reaching and worldwide significance. Christian people reading these words can testify to the drawing power of the cross. It has set us free. We have been captivated by the love of God and know that Christ's sacrifice need never be repeated. As we begin to understand God's heart of love, we cannot be satisfied that only a few should hear of it. Such love must be proclaimed and practically illustrated throughout the world.

Jesus has been the focal point of 'God's Greatest Move'. If we are truly to follow his example, we must share God's heart for lost people, and seek to bring them under his influence. When we allow the Holy Spirit to start breaking our self-centredness and replacing it with the Father's heart, we start moving out of the confines of our security. It means we stop thinking of what we want to do, where we want to go and what we spend our money on. We recognize our personal insecurities that result in us mixing with like-minded people frequently of our own age groups. With the perspective of God we start seeing people as he does. Whoever they are, whatever their background, God regards them as valuable and seeks that his love should be made known to them.

THINK IT THROUGH

1. Look at the following examples of how Jesus *spoke* to

individuals, and note your observations:

Situation	Observations	What I can learn
A religious man (John 3:1–21)		
A man with leprosy (Mark 1:40–45)		
A sick woman (Mark 5:25–34)		

2. Jesus *prayed* for people. In the following passages, make brief notes under the following headings:

Situation	Observations	What I can learn
Choosing disciples (Luke 6:12–16).		
Peter under pressure (Luke 22:31–32)		
Jesus at a funeral (John 11:32–41)		

3. 'I don't know what your destiny will be: but one thing I know—the only ones among you who will be truly happy, are those who have sought and found how to serve' (Albert Schweitzer). Would you agree or disagree with this statement?

4. Look at the specific actions mentioned in Matthew 25:31–46. What are other simple ways to help?

5. Read Romans 6:23 and 1 Peter 2:21–25. Attempt to explain these verses in a way non-Christians could understand.

6

Whose Move?

The conversation was becoming more heated. People, normally tolerant with each other, were sitting on the edge of their seats, hurling verbal guided missiles. The subject was not football or politics but the Christian teaching on election. Nasty sounding words such as Calvinism and Arminianism were used with great frequency but apparently little understanding.

'What do you mean, you don't believe in free will?'

'It's really quite simple. Everything that happens has been planned from eternity. It was all arranged that this conversation should take place at this moment.'

'And was it arranged that if you go on like that I might lose my Christian cool and do something we might both regret?'

Listening in on this conversation as a young student, I became progressively more confused. Similar discussions continue to take place. If you want to have a good meal with Christian friends spoilt, just drop words like 'election', 'predestination' and 'foreknowledge' into the general discussion. Somebody is sure to take the bait and soon there will be more heat generated from that than from the Madras curry due to be served as the main course. One way of dealing with the difficult issues involved is to avoid them altogether, but before too long someone will be talking about them again. Certainly in your reading of the Bible you will not be able to avoid the issues of God's actions in election and man's freedom.

We have observed in the lives of Adam and Eve, Noah and Abraham, that God is the initiator of any relationship. Without his activity there would have been no possibility of any intimate communication at all. The Bible is clear that 'salvation comes from the Lord' (Jonah 2:9) and unless he acts, we are lost. God, in his grace, has been active in choosing individuals and groups to carry out his purposes. What is declared in the Bible concerning election is there for our benefit and for God's glory. Although we may struggle to understand God's mind on the subjects included in this chapter, we must not take the easy way out and run from them. We do not possess the right to tell God how he should act. Our Creator does not have to disclose all his reasons to those whom he created. 'But who are you, O man, to talk back to God?' (Romans 9:20). As the Holy Spirit throws light on some of the mysteries of the Christian faith we may find ourselves appreciating more of what it means to be a child of God, and be more confident in our evangelism.

There are great dangers of either ignoring the Bible's teaching on election or failing to hold together God's action in salvation and man's responsibility. Today, as we endeavour to communicate the gospel of Christ to a generation that thinks salvation comes from man, it is easy to place so much emphasis on man, that God becomes an after-thought, available to drop into our world to meet our every need. The all-powerful God is relegated to the level of porter in a hotel—call once for service!

An emphasis on 'making decisions for Christ' being the same as becoming disciples of Christ, produces a shallowness which some never recover from. Christianity is not a sugar-coated pill that must be swallowed in order to give the individual a happy and meaningful life. Some consider that if the external packaging is attractive enough and the pill contains a coating promising health, wealth and happiness, more will be inclined to swallow it. Christianity is fiercely contemporary and there can be no excuse for presenting the unchanging message in a dull and lifeless way. When Jesus taught, he was always relevant to his hearers, dealing with issues that concerned them. While we must work hard to gain people's attention, there is a sense in which the Christian message can never be attractive. It has to humble us before it can exalt us. It has to show us our sin before we will see a Saviour. There has never been a way of presenting a cross and the necessity of carrying it, in a popular way. It will always involve making sacrifices.

If we fail to emphasize the nature of God and the demands of discipleship, we may end up deceiving people. This is not done intentionally, but happens as a result of underestimating the power of God to clearly change lives. In a success orientated world, and increasingly so in the church, the pressure is on to produce results. Those who make 'decisions' cannot always tell you what they decided or why they have decided. Such people never make it as far as belonging to the church. There is little evidence of a changed life or the power of the Holy Spirit producing Christ-like characteristics.

If our evangelism stresses man's need, to the detriment of who God is and what he demands of his followers, people will be misled. When there is a clear emphasis on God and what he has done, man's need becomes obvious. He must repent and plead for mercy.

In my early days of student evangelism, I tended to speak on the joy, peace and fulfilment available to those who came to Christ. I thought that if my presentation of the Christian faith was lively and attractive, many would respond. It was almost as if making converts depended on me. To my disappointment not many seemed to respond. Perhaps I might have made a better job of selling soap powder. A turning point came when I took a training session in preparation for a mission on 'What Christians

Believe'. The purpose of the session was to go over the fundamentals of the Christian faith and not produce converts. We hoped that would take place at the mission! Two students approached me at the end of the evening saying that they had been convinced intellectually of the truth of Christianity and now they wanted to know Christ personally. Once I had got over the initial shock, it was a privilege to help them.

As that particular session on 'What Christians Believe' was presented in other places, a similar thing happened: others were converted. There had been no attempt to pressurize people to make a decision at all. God was showing me something that was to change my emphasis on evangelism. Up until that point, I was convinced that unless I told as many people as possible of Christ, preferably in an attractive way, they would never become Christians. As I began to realize that God was the prime mover in initiating a relationship, the pressure to succeed was removed, and more people were becoming Christians! God had already been at work in the students who had come to the training sessions. They had been prepared by the Holy Spirit for that particular encounter. What God required was my willingness to co-operate with his plans, and not to force my own on him or anyone else.

Evangelism from that point meant looking for people in whom God was particularly at work. Such an approach meant seriously asking some questions about what is God's activity in salvation. The subject of election and man's responsibility, which I had tried to sidestep previously, was now back on the agenda. Before attempting to tackle some of the questions, it may be helpful to define some terms:

Election refers to the activity by which God chooses individuals and groups for a purpose.

Predestination concerns God's ability to 'decide on something beforehand'.

Foreknowledge is God's ability to know what will

happen in the future.

Calling is where God breaks through the silence caused by sin so that men and women are summoned to him and to receive mercy in Jesus Christ.

Why don't all people become Christians?

If the students referred to had been prepared by God, why didn't he prepare others? Is it that some people are so bad it is impossible for them to be saved? No! For we observe the criminal on the cross adjacent to Christ being promised a place in heaven (Luke 23:40–43). Saul of Tarsus, who had been the great persecutor of Christians and who described himself as the worst of sinners (1 Timothy 1:15), became the great advocate of the Christian faith. If the worst of sinners could be included, anyone could be.

Perhaps it is because people simply refuse to believe. Is it that when God meets such reluctance he is unable to change their minds? Surely not! God is not impotent. When we look back on our own experience, we observe a time when we lived independently of God, not wanting him to have authority over our lives. Now we recognize the situation has changed, because God has acted graciously towards us. We know that we would never have come to him unless he had made it all possible. Even the decision we made to repent and come to Christ had been made possible by God 'who works in you to will and to act according to his good purpose' (Philippians 2:13). Without his intervention we know it would have been impossible for us to be saved.

From the human perspective, we continually meet people who want nothing to do with God. Their lives are full of activity and they refuse to acknowledge that God has any claim on them. When we meet those who persistently have no regard for God, we should remember that there is also a divine side which we need to observe. In the final analysis it is God himself who makes the difference between those who believe and those who do not. It is not because some have greater opportunity to believe, or are more religiously inclined. It is not that some are more dependent people or have greater powers of reason, but because 'the Son of God has come and given us understanding, so that we may know him who is true' (1 John 5:20). God who is independent has decided to act by calling some to himself. This is his decision.

One of the clearest statements telling us of God's elective powers is Acts 13:48—'All who were appointed for eternal life believed.' F.F. Bruce commenting on this verse states, 'We cannot agree with those who attempt to tone down the predestination note of this phrase.'[11] The Greek idea is one of recording those who have been appointed to believe. Although nearly all of the city heard Paul preach that day, not all believed; it was only those who were appointed.

This had been the pattern throughout the Old Testament. At the time of the fiery prophet Elijah, a small minority of only 7,000 remained faithful to God. They had been called and kept by God himself. Although despised for their weakness by the mighty Ahab and Jezebel, God was at work in them. They were the appointed ones.

In the choosing of Israel, God chose not the mighty Egyptians or Babylonians or the cultured Greeks, but the despised Hebrews. For those who would share the intimacy of the small circle of disciples, Jesus chose a group of men without the experience and natural ability to carry on the mission of Christ once he had departed. Simon Peter was emotionally unstable and inclined to lie. Andrew had no qualities of leadership at all. Thomas demonstrated a questioning attitude which could undermine the morale of the rest. James, the Son of Alphaeus, and Thaddeus were far too radical and would register high on the manic-depressive scale. The others were unsuitable in their own ways, but all illustrate that there is nothing within any of us that makes us worth-while candidates for salvation. If there were, we could be proud and pleased with ourselves. All the praise must be given fully to the One who made it possible that anyone could be saved.

Doesn't election deny free will?

This is the question that has had people talking round in circles for years. If God is the One who initiated our salvation, are we not just like puppets on a string waiting to be hauled up? How do we attempt to gain understanding on this difficult problem?

If you want to find an answer on the basis of reason alone, your mind will be unable to cope. The Bible teaches that 'from the beginning God chose you to be saved through the sanctifying work of the Spirit and through belief in the truth' (2 Thessalonians 2:13). This verse could not be clearer, that God is the One who chooses. It does not say that because God has chosen a person they will automatically be saved, even if they don't want to be. The God who chose, appointed the means of our salvation; namely through the work of the Spirit and belief in the truth. Such action by God is the cause of fervent praise. We should not attempt to reconcile election and free will. It was C.H. Spurgeon who said that you do not try and reconcile friends.

In our own experience of coming to Christ, we recognize the events and people that particularly helped us. Looking back, we see that nobody forced us to believe and that God did not believe on our behalf. We know that we decided and we believed. Yet, we remember the drawing power of God, almost as if he put his hand on our shoulder and said, 'Come this way.' Without his help, we know that we would have gone in another direction. C.H. Spurgeon said, 'I believe in the doctrine of election, because I am quite sure that if God had not chosen me, I would never have chosen him; and I am sure he chose me before I was born, or else he would never have chosen me afterwards.'[12]

All of us who really know our hearts would surely agree.

We should also ask: in what sense do we have free will? Of twenty-two references in the Bible to 'free will', all twenty-two refer to offerings brought to God. The phrase is never used of a personal exercise of the will before coming to faith. The general teaching on man's will in the Bible is that it is far from free. If you throw a ball up in the air, there is only one direction in which it will ultimately fall. So with man; there is nothing within us that would make us choose God. The evidence is that by nature we all decide against God. We are slaves to sin. There is no possibility of persuading God to look favourably on us because we exercise something called 'free will'. The problem is not man's will, but that he will not. Sin has a fatal attraction.

If we could will ourselves to be saved, we could just as easily change our mind, exercise our will in the opposite direction, and become unsaved.

A more helpful way of addressing the problem is to think of man's responsibility, rather than free will. While there are many clear statements in the Bible about God's elective purposes, we can observe equally clear statements about man's responsibility to believe. John records the invitation of Jesus, 'Whoever lives and believes in me will never die. Do you believe this?' (John 11:26). If man's responsibility is denied, we have extreme difficulty in a verse such as 'I take no pleasure in the death of the wicked, but rather that they turn from their ways and live. Turn from your evil ways!' (Ezekiel 33:11).

God has made us responsible for our actions. We make choices every day, and are accountable to God for them. A thief may be aware of the debate concerning whether environmental or genetic factors have the greatest influence on behaviour, but when caught by the police, he cannot plead, 'It was my genes that made me do it.' Each of us is accountable for the choices we make.

In evangelism, we can describe what happens from

God's viewpoint and man's. It is always God who takes the initiative. We would not choose him on our own. Sin has too tight a grip on us, and we enjoy it too much. People are in fact exercising their will by refusing to obey Christ. The choice has already been made. There is no neutral position. Man is unable to respond positively unless God deals with him. It is God alone who can make spiritually dead men live. He can do this by changing our outlook and affections.

God, in his grace, can start changing our mind. We suddenly start taking an interest in spiritual things. The cross of Christ, which had no attraction, begins to draw our attention. We begin to realize that Christ died on the cross for sins. We become convinced that God raised Christ from the dead and that he is Lord of all. The realization dawns that if Christ had not acted on our behalf, we would have had to meet him on the Judgement Day without any hope. We realize that God has been at work and has helped us to be willing participants.

We must affirm that the Bible teaches both God's sovereignty and man's responsibility. We must resist the temptation to turn God into an ineffectual figure unable to do what he wishes because he is constantly faced by unwilling people. Equally we must resist the temptation to consider God pushing people around the stage of history, without them taking responsibility for their actions.

Suppose you live in London and are thinking of making a visit to a friend in Bristol. Finances are a little limited at the present time. There is no possibility of you making the journey unless someone provides you with a ticket. A wealthy friend purchases a ticket on your behalf and gives it to you. On your arrival at Paddington station, you are pleased that you have been provided with a seat on a nonstop train to Bristol. As you take your place in the train, you realize there are many possible ways of spending the journey. You could read or sleep. A visit to the dining carriage, or a sandwich, could help pass the time. If you wanted, you could walk up and down the train or even do a little jogging. On your journey, you have a considerable amount of choice, but your destination is secured. Through the provision of the ticket, and getting on the train, you will eventually arrive in Bristol.

God, for reasons only known to himself, has made available the ticket which will permit us to reach our ultimate destination: heaven. Nothing can stop that taking place. On our journey, we have the freedom to make many decisions. One will be to decide to stop resisting his advances. Through the Holy Spirit's ministry, he will keep us on course and make us ready for heaven. As we become more acquainted with God's handbook for travellers—the Bible—we realize that everything required has been done for us through Christ Jesus.

In the gospel accounts of the death of Christ, we can see a blending together of God's plan and the ability of individuals to exercise responsibility. The events of Jesus' life and crucifixion were known to God. They had been clearly foretold in the Old Testament. Jesus himself knew why he had come, and he walked towards Jerusalem and his death. We can observe in the background the struggles of the religious and political leaders as they decided what to do with Jesus. Pilate, Caiaphas and Herod took full responsibility for the death of Jesus and were quite aware of their ability to influence events. Satan, who had been plotting to destroy Jesus, also hoped that this would be his final victory. Both Satan and the opponents of Jesus were to regret their decisions following the resurrection, and the rapid growth of the church.

We can observe the various factors that were involved in the death of Christ. Behind the readily observable, is the unmistakable hand of God. Peter declared in Jerusalem on the day of Pentecost: 'This man was handed over to you by God's set purpose and foreknowledge; and you, with the help of wicked men, put him to death by nailing him to the cross' (Acts 2:23).

It may be easier to overstress God's sovereignty or man's responsibility because that may eradicate the tension that exists in holding both factors together. To do so, does not do justice to the Scriptures or to our own experience. Both aspects are taught in the Bible and are there to be believed.

Is God's foreknowledge the key to reconciling election and man's responsibility?

The student mentioned at the beginning of this chapter was convinced he'd solved the puzzle.

'Really it's quite easy. God knows everything and consequently he knew how we would respond when we heard the gospel. Because he knew how we would react, he arranged the circumstances to allow us to respond. Look it's so clear here in Romans 8:29, "For those God foreknew, he also predestined." Simple, isn't it, when you look at it that way!'

Although this view has its attractions, it really makes election out to be a non-event. When the determining factor is man's response, election ceases to be the particular action of God. Furthermore, the word 'knowledge' in Romans 8:29, is not the equivalent of knowing who will respond to an invitation to a particular event. It is more than a possession of information of what will happen. The thrust of the word 'know' is that of entering into a relationship with someone. We might speak of a man 'knowing' his wife. God's foreknowledge cannot explain God's action in election. It rather describes his active desire to relate to those who have been called.

Surely the consequence of election is that you can sit back and do little?

'If God has elected me, I'm going to be saved in the end, so I am free to do as I like.' The temptation to think like this is strong. Paul expected this reaction, but was sure that if we have any understanding of God's grace, it would be impossible to think like this (Romans 6). God has not chosen us for nothing. We cannot be the same again if we have been called. God's desire for us is to be like himself, and that process is going to take place throughout our life. The only real evidence of conversion is a changed life. Frequently, verses that speak of God's elective purposes also tell us of how we should live. 'For he chose us in him before the creation of the world to be holy and blameless in his sight' (Ephesians 1:4). We have been elected in order to be changed. The Holy Spirit burns out all that hinders our spiritual development, and we have a responsibility to co-operate with his activity. Sitting back and waiting for everything to happen is not commended in the Bible. In countries such as Scotland and Holland, where an emphasis has existed on God's grace in election, Christians have been at the forefront of national life. Their convictions did not lead to withdrawal, but active involvement in society.

Stressing election will result in a lack of evangelism

Those who believe strongly in God's sovereign choice are often caricatured as having no interest in evangelism. The reasoning is that if God is going to save people, he can do it quite well without our help. To think like this is to misunderstand part of the purpose of election. Men and women in the Old Testament were chosen to live for God and declare his glory to the Gentiles. It was possible for those outside Israel to enter a relationship with God. The example of Naomi's witness to Ruth in Moab is one of the outstanding examples. God required those who would speak and provide illustrations of what faith in him meant. He was at work, but required loyal representatives to carry out his purposes.

Today, we need people confident that Christ alone can

save, and who are willing to take the gospel to those who have never heard. There are those who believe in election, and those who don't, who fail to be involved in evangelism. Some refuse to evangelize because they spend all their time improving the fellowship, and others hide behind the doctrine of predestination to justify a lack of enthusiasm to see people converted. This is a result of misunderstanding and disobedience, rather than something inherent in the doctrine of election which is designed to abrogate our responsibility to evangelize. The doctrine of election can be a great spur to evangelism. Put simply, none of us can know whom God has called. People do not go round with stickers on their heads saying, 'I'm one of the elect.' We will only know who is called once they have responded. What we can do is prayerfully start observing those whom God is calling and communicate, by our life and words, the message of Christ. J.I. Packer writes,

> Evangelism is the inalienable responsibility of every Christian community, of every Christian man. We are all under orders to devote ourselves to spreading the Good News, and to use all the ingenuity and enterprise to bring it to the notice of the whole world.[13]

An understanding of election gives cause for praise because it demonstrates God's free love to those undeserving of it.

In the New Testament, Paul's teaching on election in Romans 8 is closely followed in the next chapter by his sadness at Israel's rejection of Jesus Christ. His 'heart's desire and prayer to God for the Israelites is that they may be saved' (Romans 10:1). In Paul's mind, one of the consequences of election is the active involvement in evangelism. When faced by opposition and discouragement, Paul and all the others involved in evangelism, will find perseverance and encouragement as they realize that God is at work. To be an evangelist, believing that in the final analysis what determines whether people are converted or not lies within them, must be a very frustrating experience.

We do not fully understand election, but we may accept that part of the greatness of God is that we will never fully understand all about him. We can be satisfied that the Father was concerned about us; the Son shed his blood for us; and that the Spirit is at work within us.

What should be the consequences of a belief in election?

Confidence

There will be times when we speak to people of Christ and they will be hostile and indifferent. We should not be put off by strong reactions and think that an individual could never be a Christian. When we consider our own spiritual state before conversion and remember how far from God we were, we know there is hope for everyone.

If we are confident that God is at work, we have no reason to be apologetic or defensive about what we believe. Time and energy is not wasted, as the words spoken may be words of life to someone. God can take what is said and revolutionize the life of the most unlikely person. A belief that God is at work in calling people to himself and that he has appointed you to declare the news, is a real confidence booster.

Prayer

What greater encouragement could a young missionary have than the knowledge that God is calling some to himself? How do you survive in areas where the gospel has never been proclaimed unless you are confident that God is at work? It is our privilege to proclaim the gospel of God's grace. Only heaven will reveal its full extent.

Have you noticed what happens when people start praying specifically for others to be converted? Before long, many of them are! When you start to pray evangelistically, you begin to be involved in evangelism. The prayer triplet scheme used in Mission to London and Mission England in

1982–85, proved a great help to many. Three people coming together to pray regularly for three others, saw many coming to Christ.

As we begin to pray specifically for people, we quickly realize our own powerlessness to see them change. As we pray, we acknowledge our impotence, and cry to God to act. Prayer lifts us out of the realm of human effort, into the area of God's activity. If only we could make some of our friends and family Christians, we would do everything possible to bring about their conversions. Sometimes we become so concerned about ourselves, or lazy about intercessory prayer, that we fail to ask much of God, and consequently do not receive. God keeps having to remind us that we depend totally on him, especially if we have some natural ability in communicating with others and influencing them. True prayer finds us casting ourselves on God in our helplessness.

One of the greatest joys in the Christian life is being allowed to act as a spiritual midwife when someone is 'born again'. When this does occur, there is a temptation to think we did well in communicating effectively and that we have the necessary skills to perform the task of spiritual midwifery. God quickly brings us back to reality when we say exactly the same thing to a different person and they remain far from God. Soon we will remember that salvation belongs to God, and we praise him rather than congratulate ourselves.

The knowledge that God is calling certain people to himself should make us pray fervently. We will bring to God our real concern for those we desire to see converted. Our prayer acknowledges the need of the Holy Spirit's work to change closed minds and open spiritually blind eyes. We will ask God to use our lives and the words we say to great effect. Our conviction will be that because God is sovereign in saving people, we must pray in order to be used by him in proclaiming the message. Such prayer must be specific, and have the confidence that God is powerful to save.

While today we pay great attention to the presentation of the message, we need to realize that the most difficult part is persistent praying that people will be saved. It is true that what is often most demanding is the most fruitful. If we are to see God at work more in adding to his church, we must seek him more persistently and regularly in prayer. There has been a nationwide spiritual awakening every century for the last 800 years. The last was in 1859–60. While we pray specifically for individuals, we need to pray for a mighty movement of God's Spirit to deal with large numbers of people.

Patience

The period between conception and birth is nine months. In our evangelism, we are often impatient when waiting for someone to come to new birth. We can easily be discouraged when we see little activity. Our lives are surrounded by time-saving devices and we can desire the same speed of response in the people we are praying for. Often great patience and a lot of time will be required before there are any signs of life. It takes time to win the confidence of people, and help to build an authentic picture of what Christianity is. Many we speak to will have no understanding of what Christianity is about. Over 60% of people in England have no real knowledge of the contents of the Bible. To demand an instantaneous decision about something they know nothing about, is to mislead people. J.I. Packer comments: 'Evangelism demands more patience and sheer "stickability", more reserves of persevering love and care, than most of us twentieth-century Christians have at command.'[14]

God's word does God's work. When you believe that God is at work, you do not need to tell him to hurry up. The Lord taught us the principle of one sowing and another reaping. This implies that often other people will be involved and there will be a period of time between sowing and harvest. If our confidence is in God and his word, we will not endeavour to force the pace.

When someone actually becomes a Christian following a particular conversation or evangelistic event, it is an indication that God has been at work for some time previously. Our responsibility is to be sufficiently in touch with God's time-scale of activity, so that we may be of maximum help. We must not overpress at the wrong time, or fail to take an opportunity to act as a spiritual midwife through reluctance. The midwives who helped to deliver my two children were skilled operators. They were available at just the right time.

Praise

When the Christian begins to understand God's sovereign action in salvation, it must result in praise. For some reason, God has set his love on us. This should not make us proud, but call forth from us praise. As we appreciate that salvation is a gift from God, and that we have done nothing to deserve it, we can but humbly bow in adoration.

THINK IT THROUGH

N.B. Handle this section with caution and humility

1. How can an understanding of election give you greater confidence to be involved in evangelism? Why preach and witness if the elect are going to be saved anyway?

2. A helpful way of looking at predestination is to see it in relation to Christ. God had a plan for the world centred on his Son. Trace through some of the passages:

▷ Isaiah 53
▷ Psalm 22
▷ 1 Peter 1:20
▷ Mark 8:31

▷ Hebrews 2:14–15
▷ Acts 2:22–24
▷ John 17:24

3. God also had a plan to call individuals and 'a people' to himself. In the Old and New Testaments, this involves selecting people for himself. Observe this in:

▷ Deuteronomy 7:6
▷ Isaiah 43:3–4
▷ Genesis 12:1
▷ Romans 8:28–30
▷ Ephesians 1:13–14
▷ 1 Peter 1:1–5; 2:9

4. What does Romans 9:21–22 have to say about God's right to choose?
5. Why do you think we find election and man's responsibility so difficult to hold together? Can you think of any illustrations that you have found helpful?

Part Two

Your Move

7

Your Move

Looking after a schoolboy who is only interested in finding as much pleasurable activity as possible, is very demanding. The muddy football boots are hidden under the bed. Crumpled clothes are scattered everywhere, because folding them takes time and effort. There is too much else to do to waste time being tidy. When the bedroom is in such disarray that it ought be closed as a health hazard, action is required by the boy's parents. They could plead with his sense of justice: 'We have to keep the rest of the house tidy, so you must look after your own room,' but my experience tells me that this is likely to have little effect. An alternative approach would be to point out the need and reasons why the room requires some attention, and occasionally this might have limited success. My sons do attempt to keep their rooms in reasonable condition, because they are told, 'Go and tidy your room.' The statement is not designed to lead to discussion, but action.

We have been observing God's activities as he is involved in restoring what has been lost through sin. Now we turn our attention to consider what he asks us to do. Our responsibility—to co-operate with God in the task of evangelism—is not optional, but imperative. We are to be involved because with the full authority of Jesus we have been told to.

The terrible situation of people without God, and the reality of hell, could be a motive for evangelism. We have a message about a Saviour who could help them, so we must ensure that they know it. People are lost and are in need of God's light, but this is not our prime reason to go to them. The reason for evangelizing is not the condition of man, but the command of God. We may be emotionally moved by the terrible mess that sin creates, and feel that we must help people in need. This response may lead us into contact with those in desperate situations, but it won't necessarily sustain us over long periods. Of course, the love of God does motivate us, but an emotional response to people's needs can quickly wear off or grow weary. God demands our reasoned and willing reaction. We are not to evangelize because we choose to, or we like helping people, but because we are told to.

Just as the boy is under obligation to respond to his father's command, we are given a task to perform. I used to be keen on sprinting and can remember waiting for the gun to go off. Its jolting sound would start the adrenalin pumping and suddenly the body would be moving at full speed. When it comes to evangelism, we are not to be found rooted to our starting blocks when the gun has been fired. We are not waiting for a 'word from God' to commence evangelism. The gun has been fired and the command to go has been given. Our response is either a matter of disobedience or obedience. To refuse to evangelize is as sinful as committing murder or stealing another man's wife. John Calvin said, 'The gospel does not fall from the clouds like rain by accident, but is brought by the hands of men to whom God has sent it.'

There are five passages which give us instructions concerning our responsibilities in evangelism: Matthew 28:16–20; Mark 16:15–20; Luke 24:36–49; John 20:19–23 and Acts 1:6–11. Such is the importance of worldwide evangelism that nobody reading the New Testament could fail to note what we call *the great commission*.

It tells us to go

During his public ministry, Jesus sent out his twelve disciples and seventy disciples to preach the gospel and heal the sick. Their sphere of activity was to be within the boundaries of 'the lost sheep of Israel' (Matthew 10:6). Following the death and resurrection of Jesus, a new era commenced. If it is true that with Christ's blood men were purchased from every tribe and language and people and nation (Revelation 5:9), it is essential that disciples are prepared to cross boundaries with the gospel. We are those given a task by Jesus: 'As the Father has sent me, I am sending you' (John 20:21).

The first disciples started at Jerusalem. This is where they were and there was to be no going elsewhere until the news had been proclaimed there. It would have been much easier to start away from home because of the hostility in Jerusalem concerning Jesus Christ. Feelings were running high in the city and speaking out was going to produce strong reactions. From there the immediate province of Samaria was to be evangelized. Samaria was the neighbouring province. 'The end of the earth' indicates a global mission. This was a case of eleven relatively ignorant men against the world. Who would have thought they would be able to challenge the splendour of Greece and the might of Rome? If they had gone in their own power they would have been destined to fail, but the One who sent them was to go with them.

The order is important because the task of evangelism at home and abroad is given priority. If we are only interested in our immediate locality and the support of activities we are personally involved in, we will not be obedient to the great commission. Conversely, if the church places so much emphasis on overseas work to the detriment of local evangelism, this is failing to reach our 'Jerusalem'. It is a pity that frequently people seem to be enthusiasts for home evangelism or world mission; not both. There are some who are only heard to pray for missionaries, and local initiatives receive no attention. Others give little practical help or prayer support to missionaries. There is no need for conflict between home and overseas. Both require attention and adequate resources. It is my conviction that a church that takes the task of evangelism seriously, in a world context, will be spiritually powerful at home.

Although we are frequently exhorted to 'go', few are actually involved in crossing boundaries with the gospel. Not all have the gift of evangelism, but everyone in the body of Christ is given the responsibility to take God-given opportunities. It would be useless investing money in a high powered motor car only to leave it sitting in the drive. You could make sure it is polished regularly. The manual could be consulted on how you start the car. If you were really keen, you could take a course in car maintenance. Meanwhile, the expensive machine begins to deteriorate and is waiting for someone to put a key in the ignition and engage the gear box. God cannot work through his body if it is sitting still, engaged in unproductive activities. 'The church exists for mission as fire exists for burning,' said Emil Brunner.

Being the manager of a football team at the Cup Final must be a great experience. Having spent months preparing the team, the vital moment arrives. The referee knocks at the door and the team lines up. At this stage the manager has done everything required and gives his final instructions: 'Go for it!'

Jesus had completed his personal mission. The disciples had been prepared. The command was given: 'Therefore go and make disciples of all nations' (Matthew 28:19). What would it be like on Cup Final day if the team with all the potential to win the match never left the dressing room?

It defines the task—make disciples

Jesus did not say, 'Make converts.' His command was not to count decisions, but to make disciples. The word 'disciple' is a rather important word in the gospels and Acts. We can find it no less than 264 times. The word could be used for someone who was apprenticed to a skilled craftsman or of a pupil receiving instruction from a teacher. It was not uncommon for religious leaders to have their own disciples.

The making of disciples is the imperative in Matthew 28:19. It tells us what must be done. This is the command: 'Therefore go and make disciples of all nations, baptising them in the name of the Father and of the Son and of the Holy Spirit, and teaching them to obey everything I have commanded you.'

The words 'going', 'baptising' and 'teaching', tell us how to make disciples. They are activities which help in disciple-making. We are not just to proclaim the message and expose people to its claims, but to be actively engaged in the process of making disciples. All our energies are to be directed to this end. The great question to ask of all our activities is, 'Are disciples being made?' We can often be rather proud of the number of people influenced by our evangelistic programmes, but what really matters is the number of disciples made. The crowd at the Cup Final may be impressed by the influence the centre forward has on the game. His deft touches and powerful runs into space may receive applause, but what they really want to observe is him scoring goals. There can be a lot of good teaching that is ultimately unproductive because the goal of making disciples of Jesus Christ has been forgotten.

If at the heart of the word 'disciple' is the idea of learning, it is obvious that teaching is important. Before someone can make a reasonable decision about being a disciple, some understanding is required. An emotional response to a felt need will not be sufficient to sustain the individual for the rigorous task of being a disciple. Teaching concerning the great truths of Christianity should never be without emotion. If the fact that Christ died for our sins fails to move us, there is the possibility that our nerve endings have been severed. The teacher teaches in order that someone learns. The only way we can know if we have taught anything is if there is some change in understanding and actions.

In speaking recently to a group of London teenagers, I wanted to use Zacchaeus as an example. Having mentioned his name, it was obvious that they had never heard of him. When I asked how many knew of his encounter with Jesus, in reply over 80% indicated that they knew nothing. Some understanding of the person and work of Christ and the nature of sin would have to be built up, before thinking of making a clear start as a disciple of Christ. We have the potential of disciple-making as people are exposed to the Bible and encounter Christ.

With an enquirer we are looking for:

1. A belief in one God.

2. A proper recognition of the Bible's teaching that before God, man is by nature a sinner.

3. An understanding of the work of Jesus Christ in salvation.

4. The cost of being a disciple.

This is going to take time and a great deal of patience. We will be seeking to build up an awareness in these four categories until an informed decision can be made.

We frequently expect one evangelistic meeting to hasten the process of coming to spiritual birth. Praise God for every occasion when someone has been converted on their first hearing of the gospel. This is unusual, both in the context of large-scale evangelism or person-to-person sharing of the gospel. What has been done in the previous months is vital. Simply hitting a person with a simple outline of salvation, backed up by a quick trip through the

Bible to find certain texts, will make little sense to the enquirer. What is required is the gradual building of awareness and the particular ministry of the Holy Spirit to 'convict the world of guilt in regard to sin and righteousness and judgment' (John 16:8).

When the objective is defined as disciple-making, we will not be seeking short term success. A person needs to be fully convinced that Christ's claims are true and that he is the only way. True faith comes from hearing the message, and the message is heard through the word of Christ.

Where sharing your faith with an enquirer involves dialogue and honest instruction, more people seem to be permanently built into the church. Evangelism involves responding to the other person as an individual and sincerely helping them towards faith.

Leadership Magazine, spring 1984, reports on some research in the USA by Frank Yeakley, concerning how people viewed the evangelistic process. The study identified three groups, consisting of 240 people who had received an evangelistic presentation.[15] The three groups were:

1. Church members. Those who had made a Christian commitment and were actively involved in the local church.

2. Drop outs. Those who had made a commitment but quickly dropped out.

3. No thanks. Those who said 'no thanks' to the approach made.

The people questioned were asked about the approach to evangelism. There were three broad categories:

1. Information transmission. This sees evangelism as one-way communication of certain facts. When information is transmitted an appropriate decision can be expected. It is like the lecture room approach—the aim being to impart certain information. The success of this is dependent on how many people know the message.

2. Manipulative dialogue. This approach uses a set of carefully prepared questions. The relationship between the two people involved can be likened to a salesman and

his client. The aim is to secure a 'yes' to a set of proposals.
A good practitioner will secure a high number of converts.

  3. Dialogue. Personal evangelism is viewed as a two-
way process of honest interactions. This approach cannot
be preplanned. Reaction and comment is made throughout the conversation. The aim is genuinely to help the
other person forward to an understanding of the gospel
and when they are ready, to make a response. The results
were as follows:

	Information transmission	Manipulative dialogue	Dialogue	Total
Active church members	35	36	169	240
Drop outs	25	209	6	240
No thanks	180	58	2	240

Seventy percent of those who are active members of a
church, saw evangelism as primarily based on dialogue.
By contrast, 80% of those now inactive had been
approached by somebody using manipulative dialogue.
Although there may be certain circumstances where information transmission or manipulative dialogue are used
successfully, this is not the most effective way of making
disciples. When the goal in evangelism is to help people
make decisions rather than become disciples, more are
inclined to drop out. Not all who decide become disciples.
The biblical goal is a life transformed and becoming an
active member of the body of Christ. Effective disciple-
making will place emphasis on the process rather than the
event. A decision may well be made concerning Christ and
this is part of the process.

  The discipling process does not stop when someone
commences as a Christian. The Holy Spirit is at work
changing us to be more like Christ. Disciples were not
meant to exist on their own and need to be quickly welcomed into the body of Christ. We need each other to

stimulate and at times provoke us to press on in our lifetime discipleship.

If you were a shepherd and possessed a great love for your sheep, would you entrust them to someone who would not look after them? Of course not. Jesus, the Good Shepherd, is going to entrust his spiritual lambs to those who will look after them. God, in working out his sovereign purposes in salvation, is surely looking to put those whom he has called into places where they will grow strong and healthy? There will be times when God must doubt our seriousness in praying for people to be converted. He knows our motives and is aware that when people are converted it can disturb the cosy fellowship. In a human family, once the first child is born, the parents quickly realize the home will never be the same again.

Those who are new to the Christian faith need to be welcomed and encouraged by those who have been disciples for longer. Many churches are aiming to help new disciples by arranging on an individual or group basis to see growth in at least the following areas:

1. Discipleship. How we come to be disciples. Assurance and what it involves.

2. Developing a relationship with God—including personal Bible study, prayer and worship.

3. Being a member of the body of Christ. The nature of the church and the importance of its ordinances. Understanding and using your spiritual gifts.

4. Stewardship. The continuing importance of recognizing that all our resources are gifts from God. A portion of our money and time is to be reserved for his particular use.

5. Spiritual reproduction. Living and speaking of Christ to others.

Arranging a programme for new disciples is often the prerequisite to having them. Once the initial discipling process is complete, more experienced Christians should still be stimulating others in Christian growth. We should be on the look out for those who will be particularly influenced in the kingdom of God and help them forward. The following can be observed from the discipling methods of Jesus:

1. *He was dependent on his Father*. Jesus' consuming desire was to do the will of his Father. If God is going to really use us in discipling, we must be subject to him and allow him to produce lasting fruit.

2. *He selected key people* from the larger group of disciples (Luke 6:12–16). Look out for those in the wider context of the fellowship who should be developed further.

3. *He chose people in the context of prayer* (Luke 6:12). Those who were going to be entrusted with special responsibility needed to display a real desire to follow Christ and to be immediately available (Matthew 4:20).

4. *He formed a closely knit group*. Although the disciples must have had their moments of tension together, there would have been times of great enjoyment. If you put people together for a period of time, their commitment to each other is going to develop. Jesus was prepared to spend time with these men—eating, sleeping, travelling and even sailing with them.

5. *He made clear his expectations*. Following Jesus did not mean going with a great dynamic leader. Eventually he was to be rejected and they would find cross-carrying a very difficult occupation. Those who are really going to press on need to know what is involved (Luke 16:13).

6. *He was hard on them*. Jesus himself established the pattern of openness and vulnerability. Asking the disciples, 'Do you have eyes but fail to see, and ears but fail to hear? And don't you remember?' (Mark 8:18), was hardly polite tea-time conversation. Men and women of quality can take a few knocks.

7. *He taught them by example*. You cannot disciple from a distance or pulpit. When they saw Jesus at prayer, they asked, 'Lord, teach us to pray' (Luke 11:1). They had the opportunity to observe at first hand Jesus' contact with, and ministry to, a wide range of people. This was to be

invaluable when they were launched out on their own.

8. He gave them responsibility. They were encouraged to have ministries of their own. Spiritual muscles need flexing rather than being continually spoken to. In Mark 6, there is an excellent example of responsibility being given: 'Calling the Twelve to him, he sent them out two by two and gave them authority over evil spirits' (verse 7). They were given clear instructions as to how to perform the task (verses 8–11). On their return, they 'reported to [Jesus] all they had done and taught' (verse 30). An evaluation exercise took place and they learned from each other. The disciples had been so occupied on their missions that they had not even eaten. Jesus made the arrangements for them that evening (verse 31). We can be certain they quickly fell into a contented sleep.

9. He imparted his own vision to them. Jesus always had clear objectives in mind. His ultimate goal was that his disciples should be in the reproduction business. What they had seen and heard from Jesus was to be passed on to others. Soon after his death, a whole army of disciples were on the move following a similar strategy.

10. He was always available to support. When difficulties arose, they knew who to turn to. People need encouragement and help. Jesus must have prayed many times that his little group of disciples should be very spiritually productive. Jesus' promise: 'Surely I will be with you always, to the very end of the age' (Matthew 28:20), should give us confidence to continue to look to him.

We must learn from the master plans established by Jesus for disciple-making. It was to take three years of total involvement with Jesus, before the disciples were ready to set out on their major mission. We can often think that we can adequately disciple people in three months. We have a terrible tendency to press people into some form of Christian service, before they are ready. Because there are vacancies in the activities of a church, we often expect too much of people too quickly. Thinking about and preparing people for a life of effective ministry must be a priority if we are to 'make disciples'. An unprepared conscript to Christian service rapidly becomes disenchanted, frustrated and may suffer permanent damage. Following Jesus' methods and setting up programmes that will yield lasting fruit, means we are taking the great commission seriously. The requirement is to make disciples.

It is specific about the message

Becoming a disciple of Christ is not primarily for the benefit of the individual. From being occupied with their own need, Jesus carefully and gently prepared his disciples to overcome their inertia.

They were going to have to speak openly and clearly concerning what they knew about Jesus. Their lives would obviously demonstrate the powerful effect their Master had on them. In all their contact with people, there would have been a noticeable difference, but something more was required. They must speak. Silent discipleship is something of a contradiction. Many of us are content to let our lives do the talking and hope that this will be sufficient to lead others to Christ. Obviously the example we set is important, but the great commission is specific about the need to communicate a message: 'Go into all the world and preach the good news to all creation' (Mark 16:14).

One of the Greek words for evangelism means 'to announce the good news'. Any good news such as an engagement, or the arrival of a baby, will do. It is not something to keep to yourself, but is worthy of broadcasting. The same Greek word in the New Testament is used to announce the good news that Jesus Christ died for our sins and arose from the dead. Christianity is not a large pill to be swallowed by a reluctant patient who has a problem. It is not a horrible medicine to be taken by a sick person in order to gain a future benefit. The gospel is the best possible news anyone could ever hear.

CHURCH OF SCOTLAND
BOOKSHOPS

BRANCH

  EDINBURGH

DIST   SBN

  KIO21 0860655105 FLANAGAN DECLAN

TITLE   AUTHOR

  GOD'S MOVE, YOUR MOVE

EDITION   CLASS

  PAPER   12

PRICE   NET   VAT RATE   PRICE INC. VAT

  2.25 N   1   2.25

PUBLISHER

  KINGSWAY

DATE TO SHELF

  04/03/88

Jesus' plan for his disciples was that as they went they would proclaim the gospel to every creature. It was assumed that once the disciples had accepted the need to go, they would be preaching. Mark, in his book, commences by saying, 'The beginning of the gospel about Jesus Christ, the Son of God' (Mark 1:1). He unfolds in his writing what Jesus said and did. This culminates in the heart of the gospel: the death and resurrection of Christ.

Philip—a capable mover

The evangelist Philip, in Acts 8, had just completed a very successful mission in Samaria. There had been great crowds and the message had been confirmed with miraculous signs. People had been released from Satan's grip and many were healed. Rather than leave Philip to enjoy the privileges that come the way of any successful evangelist, God sent him into the desert. Evangelists tend not to like deserted places. There he encountered a very important man from Ethiopia. The Spirit directed Philip to 'go to that chariot and stay near it' (Acts 8:29). Philip could have been content merely to allow his behaviour to act as a silent influence on the Ethiopian, but had he done so, it would have been a long run alongside the chariot! Such action would have made him like a beautiful road sign with no words on it. He had to be in a position to speak for Christ, so he did a spot of 'hitch-hiking'.

God in his sovereign purposes had been at work in this man's heart. What he required was the willingness of Philip to speak for him. Philip knew the requirements of the great commission and is a good example of the man or woman God uses to lead others to Christ:

1. He was willing to go wherever he was sent (verse 36). Philip knew that there would be times when God would require him to do things he had not expected. Whether through the prompting of the Holy Spirit within or by the supernatural visitation of an angel, he was willing to go.

2. He knew how to listen to the Holy Spirit (verse 29). A

spiritual sensitivity to discern people in whom God is particularly at work is essential. Knowledge comes through intimacy and prayer.

3. He was prepared to take every opportunity to speak the gospel (verse 30). Philip's preaching was not just done in formal settings. Any opportunity was there to be taken. Like any good communicator, he started with a question as he observed the man reading from Isaiah. 'Do you understand what you are reading?' Through asking good questions, we find out information which is essential. Frequently we want to give answers before asking questions. This usually results in the giving of stereotyped answers to questions nobody is asking.

4. He knew and could use the Scriptures (verse 35). If we have not made a careful study of the Scriptures, we will be unable to unleash their powerful potential. Philip is able to use the passage the Ethiopian was reading to lead him to a full understanding of Jesus Christ. He was not prepared for this encounter, but knew how to unleash the power of the Scriptures.

5. He directed the enquirer to Christ (verse 35). Jesus Christ is the central theme of the Bible. It is possible to point all genuine seekers to him. Our responsibility is not to speak about our church or the many spiritual blessings we have received. Those who will win others for Christ are confident in pointing people to the Saviour. Whenever there is an opportunity, we must be prepared to speak.

6. He encouraged the young disciple to publicly confess his faith (verses 37–38). The Ethiopian was going to have an important ministry on his return to Africa. He was the first known African convert and had a crucial role in seeing the church established there. An early public witness to the fact that someone is a believer is so helpful. At his own request, and before his other travelling companions, the Ethiopian declared his identification with Christ through baptism.

Philip was clear in his objectives in evangelism. He wanted on the basis of Scripture to speak the good news about Jesus. We have no reason to believe that Philip concentrated on Jesus' birth, life, lectures or miracles. Luke 24:48 says, 'You are witnesses of these things.' We may ask, 'What things?' Jesus had previously been speaking about his suffering, his death and his resurrection. He had been stressing the importance of repentance and remission of sins. The disciples were to be witnesses to these great truths. He wanted them to be clear concerning the absolute importance of his death and resurrection. This is what the 'good news' is all about. I know that it is frequently easier to speak about other things. The fact of Christ dying for our sins is not a popular message, but it is the only one which has the power to change people's lives. We must be as specific about our message as the great commission is.

It tells of the resources available

When you go for the first time into a difficult situation, it is a great help not to face it alone. To have a friend by your side is a boost to your confidence. Matthew 28:20 records Jesus' words, 'Surely I will be with you always, to the very end of the age.' The One who has all authority in heaven and on earth (verse 18) promises to be with his disciples. What a tremendous encouragement this is when you face hostility or apparently impossible situations. As we seek to fulfil the task of making disciples, we are not left on our own. The living Christ is there with us.

Christ is ever present with us because of the ministry of the Holy Spirit. The first disciples had been told to wait in Jerusalem until the Holy Spirit would be sent. At the feast of Pentecost, the Holy Spirit's power is unleashed. The disciples were empowered for the task of mission. They were not to sit around having animated discussions on the validity of supernatural phenomena, but to proclaim the good news about Jesus Christ. The disciples were naturally full of fear. They had witnessed Jesus being put to death and thought that as his close friends the same could happen to them.

John writes of the resurrection appearances of Jesus to the disciples (John 20:19–23). Their encounter with the risen Lord resulted in three wonderful gifts that are essential if we are to fulfil the great commission:

1. Jesus gave them his peace

Locked away in their isolation and uncertainty, Jesus appeared for the first time to the disciples as a group. The door had been firmly shut from the inside, but suddenly Jesus was present. At this point, the disciples must have been even more perplexed. The first words Jesus spoke to them indicates his sensitivity to their feelings: 'Peace be with you' (verse 19). The best solution to those who are afraid is the presence of Jesus who brings peace.

The Holy Spirit's great ministry is to draw attention to Jesus. Where the Spirit is genuinely at work in the disciple, there is peace. Christ gave these troubled men a calmness because of his presence.

Fear in the face of opposition leads to withdrawal. Is one of the reasons for our lack of evangelism that we are afraid of how people will react to us? The Holy Spirit has the power to turn our fears into faith. When there is an authentic work of the Holy Spirit, it does not drive us inwards, but forces us outwards. An introspective mentality is not a mark of the Spirit's activity. Today our world is mounting such a strong challenge to Christian values, it is easy to retreat to the company of like-minded people. There we may seek to cultivate 'spiritual experiences' which remove us even further from the world. Occasionally we may summon up courage to venture into enemy territory, but are glad when the time comes to retreat. To such fear the Holy Spirit can address himself. He comes not to remonstrate with us, but to bring peace.

2. Jesus gave them proof

Fear was not the only problem faced by the disciples locked in the upper room. They were also troubled by doubt. Jesus had not turned out as they expected. He was not the triumphant leader who would be regarded as a great success. He had been crucified as a criminal, not as a hero. They must have had many uncertainties as they remembered the content of Christ's teaching. For some of the disciples, doubt was moving very quickly in the direction of unbelief.

When we are filled with doubt, it is impossible to convince others of what we are saying. Unless we are absolutely convinced that Christianity is 'good news', we are going to have no real confidence in communicating it. If the gospel has totally transformed our lives, our enthusiasm for it will be obvious. Should we be uncertain of the essential truths of Christianity, or not have taken time to understand them adequately, this will be noted by those we witness to.

As we have moved progressively away from the view that the Bible is God's truthful revelation to us, the church has been sounding an uncertain note. When the Bible is regarded as only being accurate when it is true to our own experience, it begins to lose its power. We live at a time when those who see the church from the outside, perceive us as being divided and uncertain. We cannot have a Little-Jack-Horner approach to the Bible, which pulls out the plums, and leaves the more difficult pieces. Doubts need to be resolved if there is going to be any confidence to evangelize. I do not advocate an unthinking Christianity which ignores the fact that God gave us minds. Part of the apostle Paul's defence before Festus is that what he had been saying about Christianity was 'true and reasonable' (Acts 26:25). If an intellectual of the stature of Paul could be so convinced, it is not impossible for us to believe that

the risen Christ is true to our experience and Scripture.
The first disciples doubted the resurrection. Before they
could set out on their mission this had to be resolved. To
ensure that these men really had peace of mind, Jesus
'showed them his hands and his side' (John 20:20). In the
face of such evidence, and the conversation with Thomas,
they could doubt no more.

3. Jesus gave them power

It would have been relatively easy for the disciples to be
content with receiving peace and proof. They could have
returned to their previous ways of life quite content.
Something more was required. Before Jesus told them
more of what was involved, he repeated: 'Peace be with
you!' (John 20:21). These men required an extra measure
of peace, because of what was coming next. 'As the Father
has sent me' perfectly sums up the mission of Christ. 'I am
sending you' sums up the mission of these and all future
disciples. The weight of responsibility given to us is awe-
some and must not be minimized in any way. To complete
such a task, supernatural power is essential.

The men were locked in a room, afraid to go out. They
had been told what to do, but needed something dynamic
to push them out into hostile Jerusalem. Christ knew of
their need and gave them the Holy Spirit. 'Receive the
Holy Spirit' (John 20:22). Breathing on them signified that
they were being given the very Spirit of Christ himself.
This was a real gift, a foretaste of what was to come forty
days later. The Spirit of Christ would be with them until
the mighty outpouring and infilling recorded in Acts 2:
1–4.

The apostles would not have the power unless it was
given to them. They were not to speak or act on their own
authority. Natural ability or the power of reason could not
bring about spiritual revolution. The power is in the person of the Holy Spirit. It is not eloquence, the ability to
speak in tongues or a dynamic personality that make a per-

son ready to fulfil the task of the great commission. It is not through baptism, church membership or completing a course in personal evangelism that we become effective disciples of Christ. Then, as now, it is a gift of the Holy Spirit.

The lack of awareness and willingness to receive fully the gift of the Holy Spirit, makes the church so weak. The more we rely on our own ability and schemes, the less seems to happen. If you were to attempt to dig a garden with a kitchen fork instead of a garden one, it would be very frustrating. Often we go about the task of evangelism without the proper spiritual tools given by the Holy Spirit.

Having waited in Jerusalem for the feast of Pentecost, the disciples were 'clothed' with power from on high' (Luke 24:49). The same word for clothed is used in Ephesians 4:24, Colossians 3:10–12, Romans 13:14 and Galatians 3:27. These verses describe the Christian as someone who has been 'clothed' in a similar way to the apostles, with the power of the risen Christ. Although at times you may not feel the power, it is there. The word for power means simply the ability to perform. When we speak of Christ and what he has done, the Holy Spirit can take our words and use them to bring repentance and faith to others.

My car holds sufficient petrol to propel itself, with the aid of a driver, hundreds of miles at considerable speed. If the driver waits to feel the power, he will remain stationary. When the engine is started and the petrol is ignited by the spark, the power is available. We do not have to wait for the Spirit to come. He has been given. We should start to witness and live for the Lord and then we will experience his power at work.

Pentecost was the great 'missionary event' in the New Testament. From small beginnings, God was going to be on the move through his people. Boundaries were crossed as converts returned home. An army of God's people were on the move. Power had been given to fulfil the great commission. The command to 'go' remains. The same resources are available to the church today. As we move out, there will be a greater awareness of the Holy Spirit. The great American evangelist D.L. Moody wrote, 'There is not a better evangelist in the world than the Holy Spirit.'

Power given by God is the resource available to help fulfil the great commission. In keeping with the character of God and the command given by the Son, we must be people on the move with the gospel.

THINK IT THROUGH

1. Why do we need to evangelize? Consider the following possible motives. Which ones do you think are the most significant?

▷ God will judge us if we don't.
▷ God is wanting to reach lost people.
▷ The world is in a mess and we have the answers.
▷ Other Christians expect you to.
▷ God has given us the responsibility.
▷ We have been given a message of vital importance.
▷ Nothing else will change people.
▷ Life is meaningless without God.
▷ It means so much to us.
▷ We are told to by Jesus.
▷ Jesus has changed our life.

2. Look back and consider the people who have been most influential in helping you to become a disciple. What characteristics do you observe? As you share your findings with others, do you observe common factors?

3. What more could we do to make sure that disciples are built into the life of the church?

4. What particularly strikes you concerning the way

Jesus selected and developed his disciples?

    5. What is the gospel? What is essential to include?

    6. Why are we often hesitant to speak of Jesus? Look at the following verses and consider what they mean to you. What crucial elements of Jesus' life and ministry do they cover? Why not memorize them?

▷ 1 John 4:9
▷ Hebrews 12:1–3
▷ Romans 3:24–25
▷ 2 Corinthians 4:14
▷ John 14:16–17

8

Barrier Hopping

Suppose the life of a close friend is in danger. The doctors decide that the only possible remedy is through a bone marrow transplant. If this is not available within days your friend will die. You have been identified as a suitable donor. Unfortunately, your friend is living on the other side of the world and you have to take steps to reach him as quickly as possible. When you arrive at the airport, you are told that there are no seats on the plane. Once the last passenger has been counted on to the plane, it is discovered that there is a spare seat. Problem number one is overcome. You face a whole succession of practical difficulties until you eventually arrive at the hospital. The operation is successful and your friend is safe. Working against all the obstacles proves to be most worth while.

When we desire to co-operate with God and his plan for evangelism, we find many barriers stand in our way. The task of reaching lost people is demanding and we will make little progress unless we face the problems with real urgency. Barriers have to be removed in the Christian church if we are going to get on with the task. They require careful examination.

But I'm not an evangelist ...

Are you sure? Evangelists come in many shapes and sizes.

Some are fast talking and assertive; they seem to have knees fitted with anti-knocking devices. Their smile is regularly in place and they have eyes that look right through you. Some carry large Bibles that appear to be stuck to their fingertips with super glue.

Should you be very different from this popular image of an evangelist, you could conclude that you are not one. But God has provided those especially gifted as evangelists for his church, and you might be included!

The word 'evangelist' means literally 'one who announces the gospel'. It is only used three times in the New Testament. In Ephesians 4:11–12, Paul says that God gave men gifted as evangelists to the church. Philip is called an evangelist in Acts 21:8. Timothy is urged to do the work of an evangelist in 2 Timothy 4:5.

Peter Wagner in his book *Your Spiritual Gifts to Help Your Church to Grow*[16] defines the gift of evangelism as: 'The special ability that God gives to certain members of the body of Christ to share the gospel with unbelievers in such a way that men and women become Jesus' disciples and responsible members of the body of Christ.'

The evangelist will be able to communicate with the non-believer. He will be able to understand the person's thought forms and find points of contact. As we progress as disciples, it is easy to forget how we used to think and what occupied our minds. Frequently the Christian community can act like a giant vacuum cleaner which sucks us away from real contact with unbelievers. As the years go by, we become occupied with the affairs of the church to such an extent that we have no contact with those we are trying to reach. The evangelist will always maintain contact and have a God-given ability to understand what is going on in the unbeliever's mind.

Peter Wagner's description suggests that the evangelist will also have a special ability to reap. He will do more than proclaim a message. God will allow him to see lives changed. We of course must be careful of our concept of success when it comes to evangelism. What sometimes can appear to be major success, may not produce lasting fruit. Sometimes at an evangelistic event only a few are genuinely converted, but they go on to be influential for God. We can be certain that the evangelist is a little like a fisherman. He will expect to catch fish. Although he may be fully prepared and equipped, he cannot guarantee the location of the fish or whether they are biting.

Those gifted as evangelists have an important responsibility to equip the saints (Ephesians 4:12). They are to multiply their ministries through others. If the evangelist is going to do this, he should have some ability to teach and enthuse others. Enthusiasm is not always welcome, but an evangelist, if he does not switch people off immediately, should be able to switch them on.

Stereotyping those who may have the gift of evangelism is unhelpful. This results in some who have the gift not using it because they do not fit the expected pattern. An evangelist may be very effective in personal conversation, but see very little happen through evangelistic preaching. Some who are powerfully evangelistic preachers see very little success in leading people to Christ on an individual basis. Others are particularly used in training and developing those who may have evangelistic gifts.

It is possible that God will combine our natural and spiritual gifts to powerful effect. Some gifted evangelists are also effective writers. They have the ability to relate through the written word to unbelievers. They may be better at this than preaching. Those people preparing news material for the local media may well require something of an evangelistic gift.

The gift of the evangelist is there to be used. The body of Christ will multiply itself as those gifted are set free to meet with non-Christians. It is thought that around 10% of the total membership of the church will have the gift of the evangelist. It must be a priority that such people are identified and released from other tasks. How often is the

person gifted in evangelism given responsibility in other
areas of church life? If you think that you may have the gift
of evangelism, resolve to use it fully. Refuse to be drawn
into other ministries that will keep you away from the vital
task of evangelism.

Timothy is told by Paul to 'fan into flame the gift of God'
(2 Timothy 1:6). The gifted musician still needs to practise
in order to improve. Likewise those with evangelistic gifts
can develop their effectiveness. If you think you may have
this gift, work alongside those who obviously have. They
should be able to teach you many things.

Check list: Are you sure you're not an evangelist?

▷ Do you have a strong desire to share your faith with
   others?
▷ Do you find yourself continually on the look-out for
   opportunities to share your faith?
▷ Do you naturally find points of contact in your conver-
   sation with unbelievers?
▷ Do you sometimes find it easier to relate to non-Chris-
   tians than you do Christians?
▷ Do you personally enjoy talking to others about
   Christ?
▷ Has God allowed you to be used in leading others to
   Christ?
▷ Do you encourage others to be effective in their per-
   sonal witness?

If I'm not an evangelist does that let me off?

If only 10% are likely to possess the gift of evangelist, does
that mean the other 90% can opt out? There is a difference
between the gift of evangelist and the role of witness. We
are all called to be witnesses. There are no exceptions.
This is a responsibility given by Christ himself to his disciples. Because you may not have a special ability in
evangelism, it does not mean that you do not have respon-

sibility in personal witnessing. This is the privilege of every Christian – to speak truthfully of the Lord Jesus. Our lives should demonstrate the love of Christ, and the power he has exercised to effect change. We also must be prepared to go further and to speak personally for Christ whenever the opportunity arises.

The disciples in Antioch were noticed by others. The quality of their life and witness caused people to sit up and take notice. They caused a stir. Without forcing the issue, people observed those in whom the Holy Spirit lived and who followed the way of Jesus. It was other people who first called the disciples Christians (Acts 11:26).

For the evangelist to be effective, the entire body needs to be active as witnesses. So often evangelistic events see little fruit because the evangelist is expected to do everything. No one can reap a harvest without the seed being sown. The most effective method of evangelism today is what it has always been. It involves people sharing the compassion and truth about Christ with other people.

We all need encouragement and training in our role as witnesses. Regular teaching and practical help given by those who may have the gift of evangelist will be invaluable. If your church does not run a training programme, ask someone who is gifted in evangelism to share what they know with you.

Check list: The witness for Christ

▷ Are you a Christian?
▷ Are you willing to allow the Holy Spirit to work out through you?
▷ Will you allow the Holy Spirit to give you the words to say when you are uncertain?
▷ Do you have the confidence that God can use you to help others?

I don't know where to start

This is often a much greater barrier than people estimate.

Much teaching on evangelism is strong on exhortation and weak on practical suggestions. This can leave people with a sense of wanting to share their faith, but uncertain as to how to go about it. When pressure is put on to be more active in evangelism, some will end up feeling very guilty. Guilt is a poor motivator. If you are constantly made to feel guilty, it may lead to a complete cessation of evangelistic activity. 'Where the Spirit of the Lord is, there is freedom' (2 Corinthians 3:17). To find freedom in Christ, and a true motivation for evangelism, is what the Spirit would desire for us. He wants us to be his witnesses before we think about going out witnessing. What we are as people will first speak loudly to those we come into contact with.

If you are willing and available to God, he can use you. The Holy Spirit can take the most faltering testimony and basic facts that you share about Jesus Christ and use them. God specializes in using those who have a sincere love for Christ and a deep concern for the lost.

If your obstacle to being involved in evangelism is not knowing where to start, consider the following:

Start praying

Ask God to show you those he is particularly at work in. There may be some small indications of growing spiritual interest in their lives. Questions are asked. Discussion takes place without you forcing it. Become aware of the person's circumstances and start praying. There could be particular difficulties in their lives that God will need to be at work in. If there are special problems, such as objections to Christianity, marital problems, alcohol, etc., start finding out about possible ways of helping. Pray for opportunities to speak naturally of Christ. If God is at work in you, and those you are praying for, he will develop the contact.

Start building

We often want things to happen quickly. Frequently those

who are asked to give public testimony, will have experienced dramatic conversions. This is not the normative way. Time will be required to develop trust and willingness for the other person to confide in you. Do not rush. Look for opportunities to demonstrate naturally that you care. Sometimes you will fail and feel disappointed. Do not give up. When this happens, admit your failure to the Lord and where necessary apologize to the other person. None of us can care perfectly for others, although at times the unbeliever may think we should. They will be carefully observing how we handle our disappointments and failures. One way they realize that we are human is when things go wrong in our life. This information will help the person you are building a relationship with, to understand that Christianity is for failures who need to be forgiven.

Start talking in a natural way

Start speaking of the difference that Jesus has made to your life. Be honest. Honesty is contagious. As you speak of Christ, the other person may genuinely say what he thinks.

A testimony should include information concerning:

(a) What you thought and did before you became a Christian.

(b) How you became a Christian.

(c) What differences there have been in your life since you became a Christian.

(d) Some recent examples of how Christ has helped you. It can be a great help to write out your testimony. Consider either omitting or explaining any phrases that could not be understood by an enquirer. Keep a record of how God has been working in specific situations. This will give you cause for praise and thanksgiving. A praising heart will be an overflowing one.

Start introducing

Allow the person you are praying for to come into contact

with other Christians. Let them be exposed to a wide variety of Christians from different ages and backgrounds. Allow them to see the diversity of people that God has called into his family. Select people who are quickly at ease with unbelievers, and do not talk all the time! To share a meal or a social event is a good way of building friendships.

Sometimes we feel that conversations are of little value unless they particularly include aspects of the Christian faith. This is false. God has given us all things richly to enjoy and we should be able to speak about all sorts of matters. We need to ensure that we have a range of interests so we can speak naturally with other people. Christians are often boring people because they have a limited range of conversation. You may find that a Christian friend has a great deal in common with the person you are praying for. Strong bonds may be built. Praise God when this happens.

In all our churches and fellowships there needs to be special events where newcomers can be introduced to the church. Very few churches have non-Christians in mind as they prepare their services. Sometimes we should sit back and think through how someone is reacting who has never been to a service before. How much of what we do causes undue embarrassment? Do we really go out of our way to welcome guests? Is there sufficient explanation as to what is going on to help the person feel at ease? Is it assumed that everybody knows everything about Christianity? As an introduction to the church, I would want to take a friend to an event that would have a low 'cringe factor'. Those planning such events should do everything possible not to embarrass their guests unduly. The only pressure you want people to be under is from the Holy Spirit.

At some stage, we want to introduce people to the preaching of God's word. My experience has been that this is often when people are convicted of their sin and commence as Christians. We should expect to see people converted regularly as a result of direct proclamation. Those who preach should not be aiming to please the theological elite in their congregation but to be faithful to the word of God. Jesus had the ability to communicate with the common man. Following the approaches of Jesus to communication will always ensure an audience today.

Introducing people to the Bible is an important stage. It is good to have available the well illustrated and carefully introduced gospels that are available from Christian bookshops. These can be easily passed on to somebody saying, 'Have a look at Jesus as found in this gospel and let me know what you think.' This opens the way for further conversation. There are sometimes special events in people's lives where it would be appropriate to give a Bible in a modern translation. Why not write a few carefully thought out words inside by way of introduction. Some indication of where to start reading is always helpful.

Start preparing yourself to lead someone to Christ

Many Christians have sat under the ministry of God's word for years, but could never actually lead somebody to Christ. Could you really help if your friend came and said he wanted to find a living faith for himself? It does not take much time to learn a simple outline of the gospel. There are many available, and the important point is not to debate which one is the best, but to know and use one.

The outline is only an aid to use under the direction of the Holy Spirit. There are many different ways of sharing the gospel, and people's needs will vary. The advantage of having an outline is that it can be adapted to different situations. We must be willing to do this and not share it like a parrot. In your conversation you may find that someone has a good understanding of the life and work of Christ but has little understanding of repentance. You may have to major on this particular theme before progress can be made. Any outline should be committed to memory. A little time spent on this will be a blessing to you and a means of helping the others.

You may find the following two outlines helpful. First, an ABCD:

*Something to **admit***. We are sinners in need of salvation. We are all:

(a) *Sinful*. The Bible defines sin as failure (Romans 3:22–23) and as a revolt against God's law and authority (1 John 3:4).

(b) *Guilty*. Our sins have brought us under the just judgement of God and separated us from him (Isaiah 59:1–2; Romans 6:23).

(c) *Helpless* to do anything about our position. However hard we try we fail. Although we may be good we will never reach God's standards (Isaiah 64:6). No one can be saved by their own good works (Ephesians 2:8–9). Therefore we need a Saviour.

*Something to **believe***. Jesus came and died to be our Saviour. It is one thing to admit we need a Saviour. It is another thing to believe that Jesus is the Saviour. We need his ability to save us. Our trust is in his ability to keep his word.

(a) He is both God and man (1 Timothy 2:5–6).

(b) He died for our sins (Isaiah 53:5–6; 1 Peter 2:24; 3:18).

*Something to **consider***. Jesus is not only our Saviour but our Lord. Our commitment is to Christ as he is. He is to be Lord of all. We cannot pick and choose which aspects of Christ we commit ourselves to. There can be no true commitment without:

(a) Repentance—turning from known sin in the past and present (Acts 3:19).

(b) Surrendering to Christ's lordship for the future (Mark 8:34; John 13:13).

*Something to **do***. We commit ourselves to Christ as our Saviour and Lord. Our commitment is shown in:

(a) 'Coming' to Christ so that he receives us (Matthew 11:28; John 6:37).

(b) It is 'receiving' Christ so that he comes to us (John 1:12).

(c) It is recognizing that through repentance and faith the Holy Spirit has given us a gift. This is the mighty power of God which is available right from the beginning to make us like Christ.

Once you have used your outline, the person may well be ready to make a start as a Christian. Be prepared for this to happen but do not force the issue. You could ask: 'Do you think this is the right time to pray or would you like more time to consider?' It may be better for the person to go off and have a personal encounter with Christ. If you or they are in any way uncertain, it is better to leave matters in the hands of God and allow him to complete the task. If waiting is obviously the right course of action, suggest that you meet again and find out what progress has been made. Arrange a suitable time for this.

Five finger outline. This is a more simple outline which can be used visually. This outline centres on the person and work of Christ. It will help you to build up a basic understanding of what Christ has done and can do. You can easily remember this outline by thinking of the five points as fingers on your hand.

▷ Jesus demonstrates that God loves us (John 3:16).
▷ Jesus tells me where I have gone wrong and shows me how I can be put right with God (John 3:19–20).
▷ Jesus died to deal with the sin problem (Romans 5:8–11).
▷ Jesus rose from the dead and has gone to prepare a place for me in heaven (John 11:25–26).
▷ Jesus can bring about the change necessary. He can live in my life through the Holy Spirit and join me to the people of God (Romans 8:9–11).

Start persevering

You may never be in the position actually to use an outline to help somebody to salvation. If that is the case, do
not be discouraged, but keep on praying. Seek to maintain the relationship and continue to pray. Some people
will become Christians after only a short time, but
others may never come to faith as far as you know.
Never stop telling people about what Christ means to
you. There may be opportunity for them to meet other
believers.

I'm afraid

In spite of being well prepared to share the gospel, we
may never get round to actually doing so. None of us like
being rejected, as this makes us insecure. God is not the
source of our fears. We need to identify what it is that
actually stops us speaking out for Christ and then take
action. 'God did not give us a spirit of timidity, but a
spirit of power, of love and of self-discipline' (2 Timothy
1:7). Paul is urging his young friend, Timothy, to have
greater confidence in God. He is saying, 'Make use of
God's limitless, never-failing power. Fight the battle
against fear. The Holy Spirit has been given to you and
me and every believer. Do not think so much of what
might happen, but consider God's ability and readiness
to help.'

Reading and hearing good advice is all very well; acting
on it is something different. We can make a start by claim-
ing the promises contained in 2 Timothy 1:7. From there
we can go forward in obedience without being intimi-
dated.

Once you are convinced that the barriers can be overcome, you can begin to trust God. He will help you co-
operate with his master plan to reach lost people.

THINK IT THROUGH

1. What do you find the biggest obstacle to sharing your faith? Discuss the two evangelistic outlines included in this chapter.

▷ How full an explanation do you think we should give on the essential truths of the gospel?
▷ Are there other outlines that you have found useful?
▷ What are some of the dangers of using an outline?
▷ Aim to memorize key verses. Mark verses in your Bible for use in different situations.
▷ What elements of the good news do you find it most difficult to talk about?

2. We can often feel threatened by people asking us difficult questions. Work hard on how you would respond to the following comments:

▷ I'm all right as I am. (See Matthew 5:20; 22:36–40.)
▷ I don't believe the Bible. (See Matthew 4:4; 2 Corinthians 4:4; Hebrews 4:12.)
▷ God is too loving to condemn anyone (See John 8:24; 2 Peter 3:9.)
▷ I've always been a Christian. (See Isaiah 53:6; Matthew 18:3; Romans 10:9.)
▷ Why does God allow people to suffer? (See Genesis 18:25; Isaiah 55:8–9; Job 19:26.)
▷ Did Christ really rise from the dead? (See Matthew 20:19; Mark 16:6, 14; 1 Peter 3:18.)
▷ What about those who have never heard of Christ? (See Jeremiah 29:13; Romans 2:12–16.)
▷ I could never keep going if I became a Christian. (See 1 Corinthians 10:13; 2 Timothy 1:12; Jude 24.)

3. Make a study of some testimonies found in the Bible. (Joshua 23:14; Psalm 23; 27; Luke 8:26–29; John 9; Acts 4:12–20; Acts 26.)

4. The first disciples had some difficult barriers to face. Read Acts 4:13–31 and note the obstacles in their way and how they overcame them.

9

On the Move

The key word when it comes to evangelism is not method, but relationship. We have been made by God for relationship with himself and with others. When a vertical relationship is formed through faith with the Father a right horizontal relationship with others becomes possible. Because man has not followed God's design, our relationships are not what they should be. Christ made possible a basic change in the vertical and horizontal relationship.

Some relationships are deep and lasting, others shallow and fleeting. We relate at different levels to other people. All our existing relationships are the basis of our evangelistic opportunities. Without them we will not have people to speak with.

The gospel has most effectively moved out on lines of relationship. In Africa we hear reports of twenty thousand people being added to the church daily. The chief cause is the uninhibited gossiping about Jesus Christ that goes on. News about Jesus has always moved by means of relationship. Jerusalem, Judea and the ends of the earth could only be reached by one telling another.

In the twentieth century, we are always looking for something new. If an approach to evangelism is novel, people may be interested. Variety is the spice of evangelical life. There is nothing new about using relationships as our basic approach to evangelism. As you read the New Testament, you observe nothing profound—just a group of believers who quite naturally start sharing Christ with those they know. Frequently, teaching on evangelism concentrates on reaching those we do not know. We may end up feeling guilty if, when talking to someone who is not a Christian, we do not confront them with a view to conversion. Nobody likes to be thought of as being suitable conversion material. Think for a moment how you would react to a zealous member of a cult who attempts to convert you.

Any evangelistic method that does not help to build relationships will breed frustration. People often feel under pressure to produce results and simply try too hard. The gospel cannot be sold, but it can be lived.

We do not relate to unbelievers simply in order to convert them. Relationships are part of what makes life worth while. Christ was at ease with people from all kinds of background. He would be welcomed into their company. He did not have to force himself into conversation with people. Because of his openness, people would speak with Christ and they would quickly be talking about important spiritual matters. When we co-operate with the Master's plan in evangelism and move out, we can do so through natural contacts with people.

Building relationships takes time and, frequently, concerted application. The idea that this may be my last opportunity to speak to a person about their eternal destiny, can do great damage. Of course the gospel does have a cutting edge. It will convict people of sin, righteousness and judgement. We do not have to help it along by turning the sword time and time again. The Holy Spirit can take care of that as we simply witness to the truth. There are times for urgency in our witness, but the normal way will be through gradually building up relationships, which eventually may produce fruit.

We often want to say too much too quickly. We feel that

we must rattle off the most precious truths of the faith all in one go and encourage some kind of decision. If God is already at work in the person, that may be appropriate. More often, it may be better to allow certain truths of the gospel to build up gradually. When our goal is to encourage a response, we may not be listening to what a person has to say. If we are not hearing correctly, it is unlikely that we will be helping properly. Who wants a friend to always snap back an easy answer to everything that is said?

In many cases it may be easier to witness to people with whom we have no existing relationship. This is not so demanding as having constantly to live our lives out before people. But our first responsibility must be to those we are already in contact with. Every day we encounter people. Some we may naturally get on with, while others we find difficult. There will be those we find it hard to show Christ's love to, but they are there and God has brought them into contact with us. Starting where we are is the way to fulfil the great commission. We need to examine our relationship carefully, working out in a series of concentric circles.

The first major problem: you

If we are honest, this is where the greatest difficulty in evangelism lies. I do not find it difficult to be selfish. I like to keep the same circle of friends. New people are an intrusion and disturb my security.

People who have needs tend to group together. They find the support and comfort in having those needs met. We tend to feel comfortable within our existing friendship groups because it is hard work making new friends. Let's be honest about it. We all have our own feelings of inferiority at times, and a tendency towards insecurity. Frequently, the self-confident, aggressive individuals may be covering up for a basic lack of personal security. Being confident and assertive is not necessarily being a spiritual person. We tend to confuse personality and basic character. Our personality type is likely to remain unchanged throughout our life. What God does is change our character. He made you as you are. It is easy to want to be like someone else. This is especially true when we observe those who appear to be confident in evangelism. God wants to reach the world through us, as we are. We do not need to compare ourselves with others.

The Holy Spirit helps us to accept the way we are and starts building our confidence. He will show us the lostness of people without Christ. In comparison to their ultimate destiny, we have reason to be confident. We have Christ. This does not make us superior human beings, but will help us to have compassion. To build any relationship requires an element of vulnerability. When we acknowledge our sense of inadequacy, this can be the first step to developing relationships. Would you want a friend to be brash and self-confident, appearing to have all the answers? Evangelism has been defined as: 'One beggar telling another beggar where they both can find bread.'

Once you have a measure of confidence, given by God, you can start developing a plan. In our evangelism we need to be specific and to have particular people in mind. Our greatest opportunity may well exist within those closest to us.

The first opportunity — our immediate family

Family life is becoming more and more fragmented in modern society. Emphasis is quickly placed on finding a partner, getting married and usually moving away from the home base. The cycle is initiated of small families, consisting possibly of Mother and Father plus 2.2 children. The break down in marriages means that there are an increasing number of single-parent families, producing even smaller family units. Close relationships within the family are hard to achieve, but this is where our evangelism can start. Our immediate family are those we live with or have done so in the past. This is our first responsibility. If we fail to have good relationships here, it is unlikely that we will have them with people we do not know on the other side of the world.

A good example of developing family relationships in evangelism can be observed in the life of Andrew: 'He brought Simon to Jesus' (John 1:42).

Andrew had met the Lord and immediately wanted others to meet him too. The first opportunity came when he introduced his brother, Simon, to Christ. You do not read much about Andrew in the New Testament. He may not have had many natural talents, and could have been limited in his ability to perform mighty works. He did not write a book like some of the disciples. He could not preach like Peter did at Pentecost, but he could introduce people to Jesus.

Only three things are known about Andrew:

▷ He brought his own brother to Jesus (John 1:42).
▷ He brought a young boy with loaves and fishes to Jesus (John 6:8–9).
▷ He brought some Greeks to Jesus (John 12:20–22).

Largely unnoticed, perhaps unappreciated, he performed a vital task. Without Andrew, there might not have been a great preacher for the Pentecost event, Peter. Without Andrew, the hungry multitude might not have been fed, or the Greeks brought to Christ. Tradition tells us one of these Greeks was Luke, the physician, who wrote the gospel of Luke and the book of Acts. In heaven, Andrew's name will stand high among those who knew how to bring others to Christ. This is a task we could all be involved in. You may not be able to preach, sing, write or do the things that get you noticed, but through prayer and personal witness, you can follow Andrew's example.

Andrew was positive and direct in introducing Simon to

Jesus. We could follow his example and look out for at least one member of our family we could introduce to our Master. Jesus said, 'As the Father has sent me, I am sending you.'

Christian young people can show real interest and love to unbelieving parents. Through a willing submission to their authority they will commend Christ. Having a high respect and appreciation for parents is very important. We do not become superior to our parents because the Holy Spirit lives in us. Love, joy, peace, patience, kindness, goodness, faithfulness, gentleness and self-control (Galatians 5:22–23) are in short supply in most families. They are the fruit that the Spirit seeks to grow.

Christian parents will be constantly praying for their children. They are precious gifts from God, but we cannot guarantee their salvation. We will be praying for the Holy Spirit to work in their lives. Of equal importance will be praying that the marks of the Holy Spirit's activity in our lives will make us the kind of parents that our children require. Children need good examples to follow.

If, as Christian parents, you do not have time for your children because you are too busy at work or in the affairs of the church, stop. Children need to have their needs met, more than they need preaching to. Teenagers desperately cry out for someone to listen to not only what is said, but what is unsaid. The aggressive teenager is often crying out for parents who will really care, listen and help.

There is an unfathomable mystery concerning why some children are converted and others are not. All must be done to support the parents whose hearts are aching. Heaping guilt on them will only make their pain worse. If we appreciate the doctrine of the sovereignty of God in salvation, we will have a better understanding of why some are saved and others are not.

Being a good example to our children, and available to them at times of need, seem to be factors that can greatly help. When we are inconsistent and lacking in love, this is much harder. For some Christian parents, this will mean taking less responsibility for others, and caring more for the children. Being highly regarded by other Christians, but despised by our own children, indicates wrong practice.

The second opportunity—your wider family

Because of small fragmented families, we may not actually know those in our wider family circle. Sitting down with pen and paper to identify all the family links is most worth while. You may find you require several sheets of paper. Where there are blood or marriage links, there will be a whole group of people you could develop contact with. Where some kind of existing relationship is in place, seek to develop this. Find out all you can about relatives and seek to develop new points of contact. Where relatives observe that you are really interested, a relationship can be built. A new Christian can often go round quickly sharing their testimony with relatives. Often they will be surprised, but will usually give a good hearing.

You may not find it easy to develop the wider family links with your relatives. Start praying for some specifically, and observe God at work.

The third opportunity—your close friends

As well as family groups, there are opportunities to develop strong friendships with a small group of people. This may be easier than with relatives.

There was a time when I felt a little embarrassed to say that some of my best friends were not Christians. How foolish can you get? Teaching on separation from the world is important, but it must be given alongside the necessity of identification. If there are not qualities that mark us out as being different from our friends, we will have little to say to them. Should we have no identification with the world, we will have nobody to say anything to. Sadly, introspective Christianity means we frequently have little time to develop friendships with non-Christians. It is not that they are unwilling to be friendly with us, but that we do not make time to share our lives with them.

Modern society is organized with a complex mixture of voluntary associations, clubs and societies. Some are designed to perform specific tasks or for social and recreational purposes. God has made us social beings and our lives can be made more enjoyable as we share our interests with others. Natural friendships can develop in this way.

Making time to spend with other people will mean we have no shortage of both friends and evangelistic contacts. Sharing what we believe will be natural, and whether the person is responsive to the gospel or not, this should not disturb a good friendship.

A fourth opportunity—your acquaintances

Every day we are likely to come into contact with hundreds of people. Stop and think about all those people you meet during a day. Do you ever meet the milkman to pay him? Do you purchase a newspaper? Do you frequent the same shop regularly? At work do you stop and speak to others who may not have the same level of responsibility? Some of the people you meet daily will always remain in the category of acquaintances. There will be people whose faces you recognize, but you may know very little about them. Together with your family and friends, these people are within the Jerusalem, Judea and Samaria category. They consist of those who exist within your sphere of influence. They are people who are lost, but whom God has arranged to bring across your path.

Often it is people with whom we work that we get to know well. When a task is shared together, greater bonds of friendship can be developed. Simon Peter was called from the end of a fishing trip and necessary work of mending nets. Matthew was busy in his tax office, when he heard God's call. The same still happens in the work places today.

Your neighbours may not be the easiest to get along with, but given time, relationships can be built. Are there ways in which you can show your interest and concern? Love will help to meet the needs of others. Look out for any opportunity to show your interest. Neighbours may often be confused by our religious activities. They see many Christians get into their cars and drive off to church. Some might even know that we pray for the 'lost' to be saved. What they may never have had is an invitation to share a cup of coffee. How can our neighbours know we would like them to be in heaven, if we never invite them to share our earthly home? We need to get to know our neighbours, in order to find points of contact.

Society is full of opportunities for rest and relaxation. Very few are solitary activities. You cannot play snooker on your own. Even deep-sea diving is always done in pairs, although communication is rather difficult. Whatever way you choose to relax, you will find others enjoying it too. From within that group, there will be people that you could build relationships with.

The fifth opportunity—your church

In contact with every church and fellowship are large numbers of people who do not know Christ. Some may send their children and young people to church activities. Having worked hard in evangelism with many who think that Christianity is good for their children but not for themselves, I realize that this is often a hard group of people to reach. Where churches have a clear approach to reaching families for Christ, it is much easier. Our churches could do more to encourage activities for all the family. Shared activities means developing relationships. Once family activities or a programme for parents is commenced, there should be opportunities for those who are enquiring about Christianity to be taken further.

In contact with our churches, will be those among whom God is particularly at work. If you are serious about the task of evangelism, look out for those whom God is bringing into contact with your church. How sad that often those who would pray for 'souls to be saved', never actually go out of their way to welcome and befriend visitors.

Spiritually hungry people will be looking for answers to their questions. Give them opportunity to ask about and talk through their difficulties. From there, they may be gently pointed in the right direction. If God is at work in such people, we do not have to rush.

The sixth opportunity—person X

So far we have considered reaching people we are already in contact with. What about the millions of people we do not know? We cannot honestly address this problem without first being active in sharing our faith with those we already know.

If all Christians were to take responsibility for existing contacts, there would not be so many in Britain who could not be contacted by Christians.

Someone who falls into your 'person X category', may be a friend or family member of another Christian. The apostles were to start where they were and move out. Certainly they were not only to confine themselves to people they already knew. Relationship building with people we do not know at present, is vital. The ends of the earth have also to be reached.

Our responsibility for involvement in world mission is clear from the Scriptures. At the heart of God is his desire for lost people. If we are to share the Father's heart, we must be active in sending and supporting those who will be specifically called to go to the ends of the earth.

In spite of the tremendous upsurge in missionary activity in the last 200 years, there is still much to be done. Only 3% of those living in Asia are Christians. It is a sobering fact that there are more non-Christians in India and China than there are Christians in the entire world. To reach such vast numbers of people is going to take a massive mobilization of God's people.

In parts of Africa, the church is seeing tremendous growth, with up to 50% in some areas, professing Christians. There is a great need for Bible teachers and those who will encourage a lifestyle in conformity with the Scriptures. When the pressure is on, many of these new converts will turn back to their old pagan practices.

Within the Muslim world, there are 850 million people who are fiercely opposed to the gospel of Christ. After 160 years of missionary work in the Middle East, it is thought that there have not been more than 5,000 converts from Islam.

Figures such as these should not discourage us, but motivate us. The task of world evangelization can be completed. The purpose of the great commission is clearly that those living in the different people groups of the world should hear the gospel of Christ. The great commission was not our idea, but God's. He supplies the resources and the power. He gives his Spirit for the honour of his name, so that Christ may be glorified. It is a difficult but not impossible task. The resources are available. Sadly many are placed in the Western world. Ninety percent of all full-time Christian workers are located in the West, which leaves only a small number for the rest of the world. There are vast areas where people have never seen a Bible, will have never met a Christian or heard that Christ died. However, never has the church had a greater opportunity than today. The resources are available. People, finance and facilities are all there. The great question is, do we have the desire in this generation to carry on the task of world evangelism?

The God of Scripture has a passionate commitment to

evangelism. Do you? It's your move.

THINK IT THROUGH

1. List the people you could start praying for specifically in the following groups you are already in contact with.

▷ Immediate family
▷ Wider family
▷ Your close friends
▷ Your acquaintances
▷ Those in contact with your church

2. What steps could you take to further relationships with those you feel particularly concerned for?

3. How many non-Christian friends do you have? What action could you take in order to develop further contacts?

4. Consider how you could use the following opportunities to develop relationships:

▷ Birth of a baby
▷ A neighbour who has a new job
▷ You have new people living near you
▷ A person appears to be lonely

How do you think Jesus would have responded in the above situations?

5. Jesus had great skill in making contact and developing relationships. Observe him at work in John 4:1-30.

▷ Why did Jesus sit beside the well?
▷ Who started the conversation?
▷ Why was the woman there?
▷ Why was the woman surprised at Jesus' request?
▷ How does Jesus develop the conversation?
▷ What issues does he raise with her?

▷ What discoveries does the woman make?
▷ What lessons can you learn that will help you to
   develop relationships?

6. Do you feel that your church programme helps or hinders evangelism? What could be done?

7. Our personal evangelism requires thought and planning. List three starting points that would enable you to be
more effective in evangelism. Make sure that your starting
points are realistic.

8. Are there particular qualities and gifts required of the
person who will go and reach person X in a different country? If so, what are they?

APPENDIX

The Enquirers' Group

If we are to regard discipling as a process, we need to give people the opportunity to progress in their understanding of the Christian faith. The enquirers' group is set up for between six and ten people, to meet in a relaxed environment, in order to consider the Christian faith. Your home or the home of a sincere enquirer is the ideal place. The first-century Christians regularly used their homes as a meeting place with unbelievers.

▷ 'Day after day, in the temple courts and from house to house, they never stopped teaching and proclaiming the good news that Jesus is the Christ' (Acts 5:42).
▷ Paul records that he had 'taught publicly and from house to house' (Acts 20:20).

Homes are where relationships can be built. Without relationships there can be no effective evangelism. People are familiar with the home setting, whereas the church is usually regarded as 'foreign territory'. Many consider that the church is only frequented by those who claim to know everything. In the setting of a home, people are more willing to share their observations and ask their questions. Real debate can also take place without feeling threatened.

Getting started

You may already be in contact with a number of people who fall into the 'enquirers' category. They show an interest in spiritual matters and are prepared seriously to examine the credentials of Christianity. Make it known in advance that you are planning to commence a series of informal discussions concerning the Christian faith. Let people know that there will be an opportunity for them to ask any questions and to learn from each other.

My experience is that people readily respond to such an invitation if God is at work in them. Within a few weeks, you may be ready to start. Once you have established a resonable number who will attend, you can invite other friends, neighbours and people you work with, to join you. If you have the boldness, why not go to surrounding homes and invite others?

Leadership

This is the crucial factor. If you are not going to lead the group yourself, you need to find someone suitable. Not everyone gifted in teaching or preaching makes a good group leader.

In groups that I have led there has always been another Christian who is being trained to commence another group. Any Christians you decide to invite must be aware of the approach you are using and allow other people to speak. It is often other Christians who are more of a problem in the group than the enquirers. They frequently talk too much and sometimes divert conversation away from essential topics. If you are going to invite Christians, select them carefully. I have always aimed to have a majority of non-Christians present. This helps them to relax and to speak more freely.

A good leader will:

▷ Introduce people to each other and help them to relax.
▷ Be a good conversationalist on almost any topic.
▷ Be open about himself/herself and admit to not knowing all the answers.
▷ Encourage participation but not force those who only want to listen.
▷ Have an understanding of likely questions and have worked hard on providing thoughtful answers.
▷ Have a good grasp of Scripture and be able to bring the truths of Scripture into ordinary conversation. You do not have to quote chapter and verse all the time.
▷ Not talk too much (this is most important).
▷ Direct some questions to other members of the group.
▷ Attempt to avoid confrontation but develop an enquiring attitude among all present.
▷ Be sensitive to the group and the Holy Spirit at all times.
▷ Be prepared not to correct everything someone says that is in opposition to Scripture. Discernment will be required concerning what is important and what is not.
▷ Note what stage to press concerning an individual's relationship with Christ.
▷ Be available to speak with people personally at the end of the evening and possibly at other times.

What actually do you do at an enquirers' group?

The final choice of what takes place will depend on the group brought together. The leader needs to be adaptable and prepared to change his approach depending on circumstances. The enquirers' group could take the form of:

Open questioning

This is in an unstructured session that allows a free-flow of conversation on spiritual matters. An experienced leader will be required who can carefully introduce people to the Christ of the Bible.

The evangelistic Bible study group

There are a number of Bible study courses available from Christian bookshops that have an evangelistic thrust. Why not develop your own based on people Jesus met in John's gospel? You will find this not too difficult and will learn a lot yourself. A non-Christian will often give you good insights into the character of some of the people you will encounter in the gospel. The Scriptures speak for themselves so let them speak.

A talk followed by discussion

Someone who can communicate Christian truths simply and directly could be invited to speak for fifteen minutes, followed by discussion. A series of tapes by David Watson, *Christian Foundations* (Falcon Audio-Visual Aids), are excellent. This is a series of short talks given on:

▷ What do we know about Jesus?
▷ Who is Jesus Christ?
▷ Who is the Holy Spirit?
▷ Is the Bible the word of God?
▷ Why the cross?
▷ Is there life after death?
▷ Prayer

The great advantage of a tape is that you can turn it off. People often feel more comfortable in commenting when the speaker is not present.

The video series, also by David Watson, *Jesus Then and Now* (Lion Publishing with Lella Productions), is also excellent source material. It is best used with those who have a little Christian background and require a slightly more intellectual approach.

A fixed number of sessions

Inviting people to attend a definite number of sessions has many advantages:

▷ People are more likely to come to something they know is not a never-ending commitment.
▷ You may be able to have a regular group of people who will be committed to meeting weekly.
▷ The final session can include for all a summary and clear presentation of the gospel.

Some practical suggestions

▷ Men in particular seem to respond to the opportunity of talking with other men. Do not be afraid of creating a single-sex group. If women invite women, and men invite men, it has been found that more people are likely to attend.
▷ Do not confine the enquirers' group to a particular age-range. Many successful groups have included teenagers meeting with senior citizens. There is obvious scope for an enquirers'-type group being attached to church activities which are determined by age.
▷ Consider making a telephone call to remind people that the meeting is taking place.
▷ Stick to the same venue. This helps to avoid confusion.
▷ Serve refreshments as people arrive and at the end if this is appropriate. Often good conversations take place at the end of the session and into the night.
▷ Have copies of the same version of the Bible available for everyone. I have found it helpful to stick to one passage and concentrate on that in particular.
▷ If you are having a special evangelistic event, have written information available concerning the enquir-

ers' group. Encourage whoever is speaking to invite people to attend and introduce the leader personally.

▷ Anticipate and pray for some to become disciples. Have a 'discipleship group' ready to commence soon after the completion of the enquirers' course.

For Further Reading

Clive Calver, Derek Copley, Bob Moffett & Jim Smith (eds), *A Guide to Evangelism* (Marshalls 1984).

W. Oscar Thompson Jnr., *Concentric Circles of Concern* (Broadman Press 1981).

John Chapman, *Know and Tell the Gospel* (Hodder & Stoughton 1983).

C. Miller, *Evangelism and Your Church* (Presbyterian and Reformed Publishing Co. 1980).

Vernon Storr, *The Missionary Genius of the Bible* (Hodder & Stoughton 1924).

J.I. Packer, *Evangelism and the Sovereignty of God* (IVP 1961).

G. Michael Cocoris, *Evangelism: A Biblical Approach* (Moody Press 1984).

J. Kayne, *Wanted World Christians* (Baker Book House 1986).

J. Engel & W. Norton, *What's Gone Wrong with the Harvest?* (Zondervan 1975),

Bruce Milne, *Know the Truth* (IVP 1982).

John Blanchard, *Right with God* (B.O.T.).

R.T. Kendall, *Jonah* (Hodder & Stoughton 1978).

Sinclair B. Ferguson, *Man Overboard* (Marshall Pickering 1981).

John Kohlenberger III, *Jonah and Nahum* (Moody Press 1984).

John Wilson, *Pity My Simplicity* (Evangelical Press 1980).

R. B. Kuiper, God-Centred Evangelism (Banner of Truth 1966).

Notes

1. From Gordon Bailey, *Patchwork Quill* (SOL Publications 1975).
2. W.N. Clarke, *The Christian Doctrine of God* (T. & T. Clark, 1912), p.26.
3. From 'Jonah', *Illustrated Bible Dictionary* (IVP 1980), p.807.
4. See Genesis 22:18; Exodus 12:49; Leviticus 19:34; 1 Kings 8:41–43; Ezra 6:21; Psalm 72:8–17; Isaiah 54:2; Jeremiah 39:15–18; Joel 29:28–32; Amos 9:11–12; Zechariah 8:23; Malachi 1:11.
5. R.V.G. Tasker, *Matthew* (IVP 1983), p.217.
6. *UK Christian Handbook 1985/86* (MARC Europe), p.27.
7. Ibid.
8. Ibid.
9. P. Johnstone, *Operation World* (STL/WEC 1986), p.35.
10. John Stott, *The Cross of Christ* (IVP 1986), p.216.
11. F.F. Bruce, *The Book of Acts* (Marshall Morgan & Scott 1954), p.283.
12. From John Blanchard, *Gathered Gold* (Evangelical Press), p.78.
13. J.I. Packer, *Evangelism and the Sovereignty of God* (IVP 1961), p.26.
14. Ibid., p.120.
15. W. & C. Arn, 'Closing the Back Door', *Leadership Magazine* (Spring 1984), p.26.
16. Peter Wagner, *Your Spiritual Gifts Can Make Your Church Grow* (Regal Books 1982), p.262.